NEW REVISED

CAMBRIDGE

GED
PROGRAM

EXERCISE BOOK FOR **Mathematics**

N. Y. S. T. L.
Property of
Offsite Educational Services

CAMBRIDGE ADULT EDUCATION
A Division of Simon & Schuster
Upper Saddle River, New Jersey

NEW REVISED CAMBRIDGE GED PROGRAM

WRITERS
Beverly Ann Chin
Gloria Levine
Karen Wunderman
Stella Sands
Michael Ross
Alan Hines
Donald Gerstein

CONSULTANTS/REVIEWERS
Marjorie Jacobs
Cecily Bodnar
Diane Hardison
Dr. Margaret Tinzmann
Nora Chomitz
Bert C. Honigman
Sylvester Pues

COVER
Art Director: Josée Ungaretta
Cover Design: Marta Wolchuk, Design Five, NYC
Cover Illustration: Min Jae Hong

Copyright © 1994, 1998 by Globe Fearon, Inc. A Simon & Schuster Company. One Lake Street, Upper Saddle River, New Jersey 07458. All rights reserved. No part of this book may be reproduced or transmitted in any form or by any means, electronic, photographic, mechanical, or otherwise, including photocopying, recording, or by any information storage and retrieval system, without permission in writing from the publisher.

Printed in the United States of America

4 5 6 7 8 9 10   01 00

ISBN 0-835-94743-2

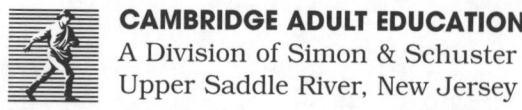

CAMBRIDGE ADULT EDUCATION
A Division of Simon & Schuster
Upper Saddle River, New Jersey

Contents

Chapter 1 Whole Numbers 1
    Level 1   Whole Number Skills 1
    Level 2   Whole Number Application 2
    Level 3   Whole Number Problem Solving 5

Chapter 2 Decimals 11
    Level 1   Decimals Skills 11
    Level 2   Decimals Application 12
    Level 3   Decimals Problem Solving 15

Chapter 3 Fractions 21
    Level 1   Fractions Skills 21
    Level 2   Fractions Application 22
    Level 3   Fractions Problem Solving 25

Chapter 4 Percents 29
    Level 1   Percents Skills 29
    Level 2   Percents Application 30
    Level 3   Percents Problem Solving 32

Chapter 5 Graphs 37

Chapter 6 Algebra 47
    Level 1   Algebra Skills 47
    Level 2   Algebra Application 48
    Level 3   Algebra Problem Solving 50

Chapter 7 Geometry 55
    Level 1   Geometry Skills 55
    Level 2   Geometry Application 57
    Level 3   Geometry Problem Solving 61

Half-Length Practice Test 67
    Performance Analysis Chart 73

Full-Length Practice Test 75
    Performance Analysis Chart 85

Simulated Test 87
    Performance Analysis Chart 96

Answers and Explanations 97
    Chapters 1-7 97
    Half-Length Practice Test 129
    Full-Length Practice Test 131
    Simulated Test 134

Formulas 139

Introduction

This *Exercise Book for the Mathematics Test* can help you prepare for the Mathematics Test of the GED. You can use it along with either the *New Revised Cambridge GED Program: Comprehensive Book* or the *New Revised Cambridge GED Program: Mathematics*.

The Three Sections of this Book

This book has three sections: Exercise, Practice, and Simulation. All three sections share a common purpose–to provide you with practice on the mathematics skills that you need when you take the GED. The paragraphs that follow explain what each section of this book is and tell you how to use them to your best advantage.

The Exercise Section

What is the Exercise Section? The Exercise Section (Chapters 1–7) allows you to practice one area of mathematics at a time. It is made up of mathematics activities grouped according to the levels in the math instruction section of the *New Revised Cambridge Ged Program: Mathematics* and in Unit V of the *New Revised Cambridge GED Program: Comprehensive Book*. There is a group of exercises for each level of each chapter in either book. The Level 1 Exercises in Basic Skills are all non-multiple choice questions. The Level 2 Exercises in Application and the Level 3 Exercises in Problem Solving contain a mixture of multiple-choice and non-multiple choice questions.

How to Use the Exercise Section. After you complete a level in either of the Cambridge texts, you can practice by using the corresponding Exercises in this book. This allows you to practice with skills you have just studied in order to reinforce them. But, if you want to, you can wait until after you've studied a whole chapter of instruction and then complete the related Exercises to test several math skills at once. It would probably be best for you to complete the Exercise in this book before you work on the corresponding Practice section in the textbooks.

The Practice Tests

What are the Practice Tests? This book has two Practice Tests that are structured like the actual Mathematics Test of the GED. The types of math you need to use vary from item to item, just as on the real test. The first test, called Half-Length Practice Test, is made up of 28 items–half as many as on the actual GED. The second practice test is full length, the same length as the real test. Both tests give you an opportunity to practice taking a test similar to the GED.

How to Use the Practice Tests. You should take the practice tests after you have completed the math instruction section in a Cambridge text and the exercises in this book. It would probably be best to take the practice tests in this book after you complete the Practice section in either text. The Half-Length Practice Test should take 45 minutes. The Full-Length Practice test should take 90 minutes, the same amount of time allowed on the actual GED test.

The Simulated Test

What is the Simulated Test? The Simulated Test is as much like the actual GED test as possible. It has the same number of questions and is just as challenging as the real test. As on the practice tests, the type of math skill you need to apply varies from item to item. Taking the Simulated Test will help you determine how ready you are to take the real GED test.

How to Use the Simulated Test. You can take the Simulated Test before or after you've taken the Simulated Math Test in one of the Cambridge texts. Take the Simulated Test under the same conditions as you will have when you take the real Mathematics Test–work without interruption and do not talk to anyone or consult any other materials. You should complete the Simulated Test in 90 minutes, the same amount of time you will have on the actual GED.

Scoring Your Work and Using Your Scores

You will find that the Answers and Explanations is a very useful study tool. When you complete a section in this book, compare your answers to the correct answers in Answers and Explanations. Whether you answer an item correctly or not, you should read through the Answers and Explanations. Doing this will reinforce your ability with mathematics and develop your test-taking skills.

After you check your answers with the items on one of the three tests, you can complete the appropriate Performance Analysis Chart. The charts can help you determine which math skills and problem types you are strongest in, and direct you to parts of the Cambridge texts where you can review areas in which you need additional work.

Chapter 1

Whole Numbers

Level 1 — Whole Number Skills

1. In the number 3,507,462, which digit is in the hundred thousands place?

2. In the number 6,924,317, which digit is in the thousands place?

3. What is the value of 7 in the number 326,704?

4. What is the value of 6 in the number 6,004,521?

5. What is the value of 9 in the number 7,295,436?

6. What is the product of 59 times 47?

7. What is the difference between 6003 and 926?

8. What is the quotient of 504 divided by 21?

9. Subtract 4932 from 15,800.

10. Find the quotient of 1061 divided by 429.

11. What is the sum of 364, 855, 32, and 678?

12. Find the product of 3807 and 72.

13. Simplify the following: 86 + 9440 + 302 + 51,394.

14. Simplify $\dfrac{5888}{32}$.

15. Find the difference between 52,004 and 43,997.

16. What is the product of 974 times 639?

17. Which of the following is the correct setup to find the difference between 9614 and 439?

    (1) $\quad\begin{array}{r} 439 \\ +\ 9614 \end{array}$

    (2) $\quad\begin{array}{r} 439 \\ -\ 9614 \end{array}$

    (3) $\quad\begin{array}{r} 9614 \\ +\ 439 \end{array}$

    (4) $\quad\begin{array}{r} 9614 \\ -\ 439 \end{array}$

    (5) $\quad\begin{array}{r} 9614 \\ -\ 439 \end{array}$

18. Which of the following is the correct setup to find the product of 382 and 61?

    (1) $\quad\begin{array}{r} 382 \\ +\ 61 \end{array}$

(2)   382
      ×   61

(3)   382
      −   61

(4)   61)382

(5) 382)61

19. Which of the following is the correct setup to find the quotient of 3060 divided by 85?

(1)   85
     + 3060

(2)   3060
     ×   85

(3)   3060
     −   85

(4)   85)3060

(5) 3060)85

20. Which of the following is the correct setup to find the sum of 96, 704, and 8?

(1)   96
     704
   +   8

(2)   96
     704
   + 80

(3)   96
     704
   +   8

(4)   96
     704
   +   8

(5)   960
     704
   + 800

Check your answers starting on page 97.

Level 2
Whole Number Application

1. Obtuseville has a population of 24,643 persons. What is its population to the nearest thousand?

2. The Obtuseville police department has an annual budget of $6,749,000. What is its budget to the nearest hundred thousand?

3. Melissa Bulaka drove for 6 hours at 59 miles an hour. How many miles did she drive?

4. Henry's Office Supplies purchased 24 boxes of computer floppy disks at a cost of $13 per box. What was the total cost of this purchase?

5. Rose owns a flower shop. On Monday, she had 90 customers; Tuesday, 81 customers; Wednesday, 116 customers; Thursday, 78 customers; and Friday, 125 customers. Find the daily mean number of customers she had during this 5-day period.

Chapter 1: Whole Numbers

6. What was the daily median number of customers for the shop described in item 5?

7. What is the value of 8^4?

8. What is the value of $2^3 + 3^4$?

9. What is the square root of 729?

10. What is the perimeter of the triangle shown below?

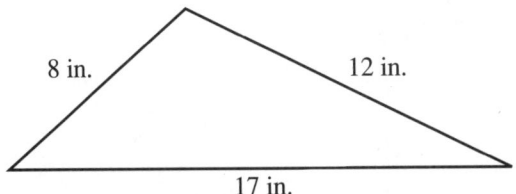

11. What is the perimeter of the rectangle shown below?

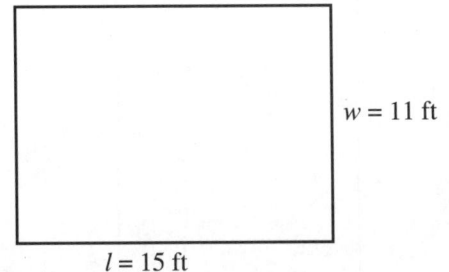

12. What is the perimeter of a square whose side is 23 centimeters?

13. What is the area of a rectangle with a length of 12 meters and a width of 8 meters?

14. What is the area of the square shown below?

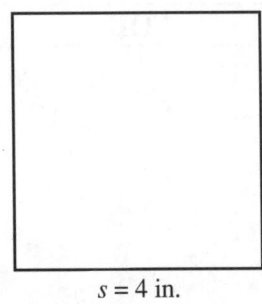

15. What is the volume in cubic inches of the cereal box shown below?

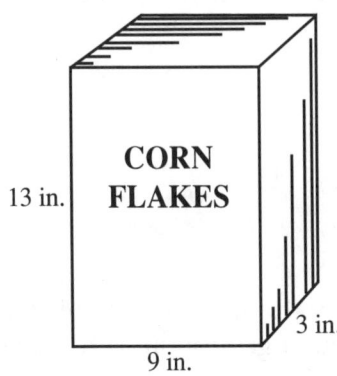

16. What is the volume of a cube with a side of 7 feet?

17. The revenues of National Manufacturing, Inc. for last year total $383,252,165. What are the company's revenues rounded to the nearest million?

   (1) $380,000,000
   (2) $383,000,000
   (3) $383,300,000
   (4) $384,000,000
   (5) $400,000,000

18. The Wagners drove at an average speed of 53 miles per hour for 20 hours on their vacation. How many miles did they drive?

   (1) 73
   (2) 550
   (3) 1060
   (4) 2120
   (5) 3180

19. At $0.47 per pound, what is the cost of 4 pounds of bananas?

   (1) $0.12
   (2) $0.51
   (3) $1.68
   (4) $1.88
   (5) $4.47

Chapter 1, Level 2

20. Bertha Mandlin's grandchildren are ages 4, 12, 19, 2, 6, 4, 17, and 8. What is the mean age of her grandchildren?

(1) 8
(2) 9
(3) 11
(4) 12
(5) 15

21. What is the median age of Bertha Mandlin's grandchildren described in item 20?

(1) 2
(2) 4
(3) 6
(4) 7
(5) 8

22. What is the value of $3^2 + 4^0 - 5^1$?

(1) 1
(2) 2
(3) 5
(4) 8
(5) 12

23. What does $\sqrt{5929}$ equal?

(1) 32
(2) 49
(3) 77
(4) 84
(5) 96

24. What is the perimeter in inches of the picture frame shown below?

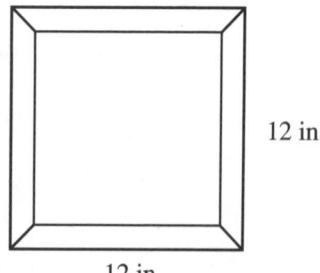

(1) 16
(2) 24
(3) 48

(4) 96
(5) 144

25. What is the perimeter in feet of the garden shown below?

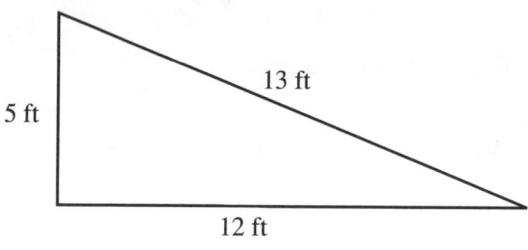

(1) 30
(2) 34
(3) 36
(4) 156
(5) 780

26. How many square feet of carpeting are needed to cover the area shown below?

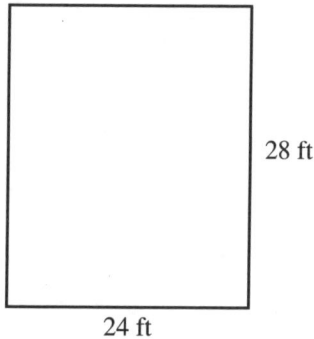

(1) 104
(2) 112
(3) 324
(4) 576
(5) 672

27. What is the volume in cubic inches of the foil box shown below?

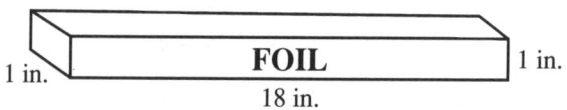

(1) 18
(2) 20
(3) 40
(4) 36
(5) 72

Chapter 1: Whole Numbers

28. Which of the following is the same as 5×12?

- (1) $5 + 12$
- (2) $12 + 5$
- (3) $12 - 5$
- (4) 12×5
- (5) $12 \div 5$

29. Choose the expression that equals $4 + (6 + 7)$.

- (1) $4(6 + 7)$
- (2) $(4 + 6) + 7$
- (3) $(4 + 6) \times 7$
- (4) $4 + 6 + 4 + 7$
- (5) $4 \times 6 + 4 \times 7$

30. Which of the following expressions equals $27(8 - 1)$?

- (1) $27(8) - 27(1)$
- (2) $27(8) + 27(1)$
- (3) $27(1) + 27(8)$
- (4) $27(1) - 27(8)$
- (5) $8(27) + 1(27)$

Check your answers starting on page 97.

Level 3 — Whole Number Problem Solving

1. The Wings' total expenses for one month were the following: house payment, $525; car payment, $182; food, $247; clothing, $176; and utilities, $118. What were their total expenses for the month?

2. Sue Tornelli bought a dress at a clearance sale for $67. The dress originally cost $105. How much less than the original price did she pay?

3. Randall Jesse, Herman Mansky, Sean Cornell, and Jane Burke are partners in a record store. The store's profits for one month were $4188. If they share the profits evenly, how much will each person receive?

4. Francine Verkett works 8 hours each day as a receptionist. She answers an average of 18 phone calls each hour. At this rate, how many phone calls does she answer each day?

5. Brad Knowland needs to buy fencing to enclose his vegetable garden. The garden is 36 feet long and 56 feet wide. Find the distance around his garden.

6. Noeliton has a population of 157,393 people. If each household has an average of 4 persons in it, approximately how many households are there in Noeliton?

7. The Rialto Theater had the following ticket sales for 5 consecutive days: Monday, 310; Tuesday, 291; Wednesday, 422; Thursday, 538; Friday, 687. How many tickets were sold for this 5-day period?

8. Wanda Druckett earned $18,949 one year and $23,091 the next. How much more money did she earn in the second year?

9. To get to her brother's house, Lisa Piquane drove at 44 miles per hour for 2 hours on Route 15 and 5 hours at 52 miles per hour on Route 60. How many miles did she drive?

10. One week Morris Dreednerton worked 38 hours at $7 per hour. The next week he worked 39 hours at $12 per hour. What was his average weekly salary for this 2-week period?

11. During a shopping trip to a department store, Marian Leotini purchased a $25 shirt that was marked down $6, a $34 pair of pants that was marked down $9, and 3 pairs of $4 stockings that were marked down $1. What was the total cost of her purchases?

12. What is the area of the figure shown below?

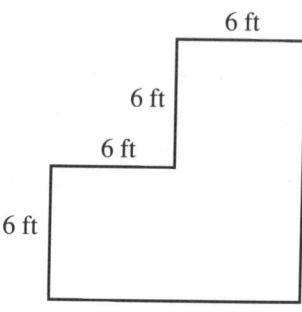

13. What is the area of the shaded portion of the figure shown below?

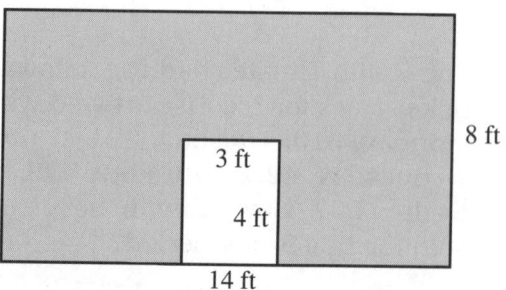

Items 14 and 15 are based on the following table.

AROUND THE WORLD			
	HI	LOW	SKY
Amsterdam	55	50	cdy
Athens	61	50	cdy
Bangkok	84	70	clr
Barbados	84	73	cdy
Beirut	70	57	clr
Belgrade	50	41	cdy
Berlin	54	48	cdy
Bermuda	73	66	cdy
Bogota	68	50	cdy
Brussels	54	43	cdy
Buenos Aires	71	59	rn
Cairo	75	57	clr
Caracas	79	63	cdy
Copenhagen	46	43	cdy
Dublin	59	45	rn
Frankfurt	50	45	cdy
Geneva	48	32	clr
Havana	90	73	clr
Helsinki	43	39	rn
Hong Kong	70	66	cdy
Istanbul	59	48	cdy
Jerusalem	64	45	cdy

14. Which city had the lowest high temperature?

15. What is the difference in degrees between the high and the low temperatures recorded in Cairo?

Items 16 to 19 are based on the following information.

A patent gives a person protection from anyone using or copying his or her invention. In the United States patents are issued by the U.S. Patent Office, which was established in 1836.

In one year 100,000 patent applications were received. Of the 78,304 patents issued, 54,960 were issued to U.S. citizens; the rest were issued to citizens of foreign countries.

The following fees are charged when applying for a patent: filing fee, $65; issue fee, $100; and printing fee, $70. Often an inventor also employs a patent attorney. The attorney's fee is $500.

A patent is good for 17 years. Once a patent is granted, it can be sold or licensed to a manufacturer.

6   Chapter 1: Whole Numbers

16. In 1992, how many years had the patent office been in operation?

17. Of the patent applications received in one year, how many were not granted?

18. If an inventor uses a patent attorney, what will be the total cost of applying for a patent?

19. Warren Puchilski licensed his invention for $7856 a year for the first 12 years of the patent, and $9289 a year for the remaining years. How much money will he earn in all over the life of the patent?

20. Dave made a gross salary of $1360 last month. His employer deducted $408 from his salary for taxes and insurance. What was Dave's net salary for the month?

    (1) $ 272
    (2) $ 333
    (3) $ 952
    (4) $1168
    (5) $1768

21. Robin Harchert saved $1820 in one year. If she deposited the same amount into her account every week, how much did she deposit each week?

    (1) $ 35
    (2) $ 52
    (3) $ 73
    (4) $ 78
    (5) $102

22. A packing crate is 2 feet long, 2 feet wide, and 3 feet deep. What is the capacity of the crate in cubic feet?

    (1) 4
    (2) 6
    (3) 7
    (4) 12
    (5) 24

23. Walter Wagner purchased a new car for $7894. Sales tax and license plates increased the price $1052. What was the approximate total price?

    (1) $ 6000
    (2) $ 7000
    (3) $ 8000
    (4) $ 9000
    (5) $10,000

24. On a given day last year 26,245 people had jobs in a certain area. On the same day this year 43,478 people had jobs in the same area. Approximately how many more people were employed this year than last year?

    (1) 17,000
    (2) 18,000
    (3) 19,000
    (4) 170,000
    (5) 180,000

25. Brenda Mentmore planted 325 acres of corn. The average yield per acre was 17 bushels. Approximately how many bushels of corn did Brenda harvest?

    (1) 60
    (2) 600
    (3) 6000
    (4) 60,000
    (5) 600,000

26. Rhonda Phister's car holds 15 gallons of gasoline and can be driven 18 miles on one gallon of gas. Brad Shonnoff's car holds 12 gallons and can go 25 miles on one gallon of gas. How many miles farther than Rhonda's car can Brad's car be driven on a full tank of gas?

    (1) 3
    (2) 7
    (3) 23
    (4) 30
    (5) 37

27. Two employees at the Warbler Company earn $6 per hour, 6 employees earn $8 per hour, and 4 employees earn $12 per hour. What is the company's average hourly pay rate?

(1) $ 6
(2) $ 8
(3) $ 9
(4) $12
(5) $24

28. Peter DeCerro set up 29 rows of 15 chairs each for a concert. If 296 people attended the concert, how many chairs were empty?

(1) 106
(2) 139
(3) 200
(4) 296
(5) 435

29. What is the combined area in square feet of the walk and patio shown below?

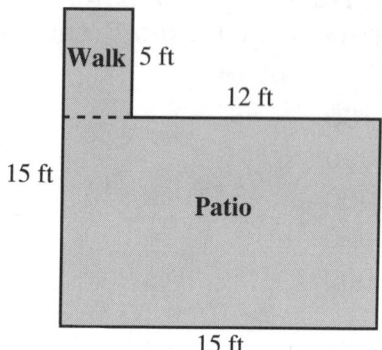

(1) 135
(2) 150
(3) 165
(4) 185
(5) 225

Items 30 and 31 are based on the following table.

DAILY SALES	
Sunday	$502
Monday	490
Tuesday	317
Wednesday	760
Thursday	818
Friday	678
Saturday	941

30. Which day had the median sales for the week shown in the table?

(1) Sunday
(2) Monday
(3) Tuesday
(4) Wednesday
(5) Friday

31. How much more were the sales on Friday than on Monday?

(1) $ 12
(2) $ 188
(3) $ 228
(4) $ 263
(5) $1168

Items 32 and 33 are based on the following information.

A furniture dealer sells conventional beds and waterbeds. The conventional beds come in four sizes: bunk at $49, twin at $87, queen at $318, and king at $527. The waterbeds also come in four sizes, plus three types of firmness. The sizes are single, double, queen, and king. All sizes are priced the same for the same firmness. The prices for each type of firmness are wavy at $109, semi-waveless at $170, and waveless at $349.

32. If the furniture dealer purchases eight conventional queen-size mattresses for $229 and sells them all at the regular price, what will be his net profit?

(1) $ 89
(2) $ 642

Chapter 1: Whole Numbers

(3) $ 712
(4) $1832
(5) $2544

33. If in one day the dealer sold one conventional bunk bed, one conventional twin bed, one conventional queen-size bed, and one double semiwaveless waterbed, what were his average sales that day?

   (1) $151
   (2) $156
   (3) $170
   (4) $245
   (5) $624

34. Last year Yvonne Garland could bench-press 145 pounds. This year she can bench-press 178 pounds. Which of the following expressions shows the increase in the amount she can press?

   (1) $145 + 178$
   (2) $145 - 178$
   (3) 145×178
   (4) $178 - 145$
   (5) $\dfrac{178}{145}$

35. Joan Walker works 40 hours a week and earns $498 a week. A total of $182 is deducted. Which of the following expressions represents her net hourly wage?

   (1) $40 + 498 - 182$
   (2) $40(498 - 182)$
   (3) $498 - \dfrac{182}{40}$
   (4) $\dfrac{498}{40} - 182$
   (5) $\dfrac{498 - 182}{40}$

36. Diane Nuigen wants to carpet a rectangular room measuring 4 yards by 5 yards. If the carpet she wants costs $12 per square yard, which of the following expresses the cost of carpeting the room?

   (1) $\dfrac{4 \times 5}{12}$
   (2) $12(4 + 5)$
   (3) $12(4 \times 5)$
   (4) $\dfrac{12}{4 \times 5}$
   (5) $12(2 \times 4 + 2 \times 5)$

37. Milton Bruick has $685 in his checking account. He wrote checks for $21, $98, $66, and $182. Which of the following expressions would show how much money he would have remaining in his checking account?

   (1) $685 + 21 + 98 + 66 + 182$
   (2) $(21 + 98 + 66 + 182) - 685$
   (3) $685 - (21 + 98 + 66 + 182)$
   (4) $685 + (21 + 98 + 66 + 182)$
   (5) $685(21 + 98 + 66 + 182)$

38. One edition of a newspaper had 122 pages. A total of 8876 pages can be printed on one roll of newsprint. If 347,984 newspapers were printed, which of the following expressions would show how many rolls of newsprint were used?

   (1) $\dfrac{347,984}{8876}$
   (2) 8876×122
   (3) $\dfrac{8876 \times 122}{347,984}$
   (4) $\dfrac{347,984 \times 122}{8876}$
   (5) $347,984 \times 122 \times 8876$

39. Matilda Larson bought a 20-pound turkey costing $2 per pound and five dozen doughnuts at $3 per dozen. Which of the following expressions shows her total cost?

    (1) $20(2)+5(3)$
    (2) $20(2)-5(3)$
    (3) $20(2) \times 5(3)$
    (4) $(20+5)(2+3)$
    (5) $(20+5)+(2+3)$

40. Wyatt Numbton put $466 down on a new car and made 48 monthly payments of $356 each to pay the balance. Which of the following expressions shows the total cost of the car?

    (1) $48(466+356)$
    (2) $48(466-356)$
    (3) $48(466)+356$
    (4) $48(356)+466$
    (5) $48(356)-466$

Check your answers starting on page 99.

Chapter 2

Decimals

Level 1 — Decimals Skills

1. In 0.1395, which digit is in the thousandths place?

2. In 26.8403, which digit is in the hundredths place?

3. Write 0.086 in word form.

4. Write five and six hundred thirty-five millionths as a mixed decimal.

5. Write 30.0476 in word form.

6. Write nine thousand twenty-one hundred-thousandths as a decimal.

7. Find the sum of 5.02, 0.51, and 0.6.

8. Find the difference between 11.92 and 2.455.

9. What is the product of 0.105 times 0.44?

10. What is the quotient of 0.01011 divided by 3?

11. Divide 55 by 0.11.

12. What is the quotient of 0.5448 divided by 0.06?

13. Add 11.876, 5, and 5.3.

14. Find the product of 12.5×0.08.

15. Subtract 0.019 from 3.

16. What is 208 divided by 0.64?

17. Find the quotient of 0.0156 divided by 0.012.

18. Which is larger, 0.03 or 0.014?

19. Arrange 0.27, 0.027, 0.207, and 0.2 in order from smallest to largest.

20. Arrange 8.4, 8.045, 8.405, and 8.05 in order from largest to smallest.

Check your answers starting on page 101.

Level 2

Decimals Application

1. What is 0.5783 rounded to the nearest thousandth?

2. Change 0.324 meter to millimeters.

3. Change 4650 milligrams to grams.

Items 4 and 5 are based on the 10-centimeter ruler shown below.

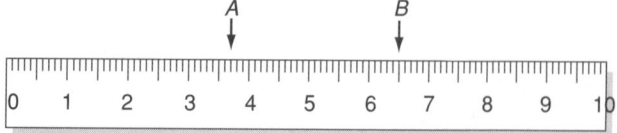

4. How far from the left end of the ruler is point A?

5. What is the distance between points A and B on the ruler?

6. What does 0.08^2 equal?

7. What is the square root of 0.000144?

8. What is the circumference of the circle shown below?

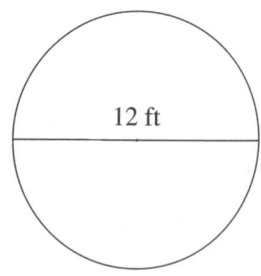

9. What is the area of the circle shown below?

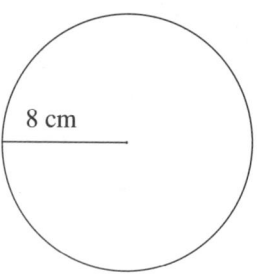

10. What is the volume of the cylinder shown below?

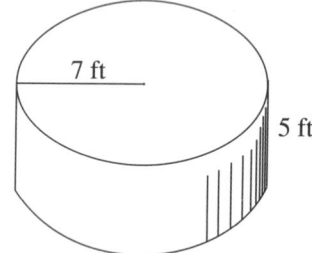

11. Find the perimeter of the triangle shown below.

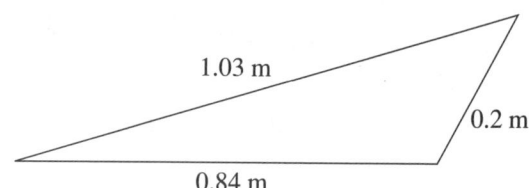

12. What is the area of the rectangle shown below?

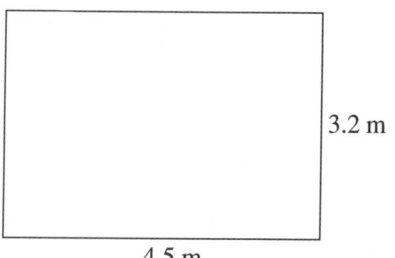

12   Chapter 2: Decimals

13. What is the volume of the box shown below?

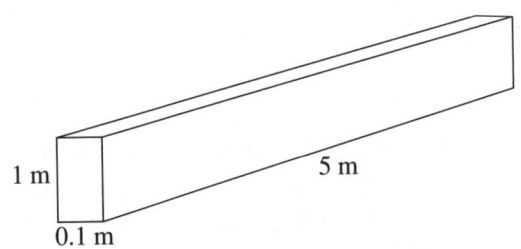

14. Bernard bought 9.8 gallons of gasoline for $1.129 per gallon. How much did it cost him? (Be sure to round your answer to the nearest cent.)

15. Mary bought five pieces of fabric on sale. One piece was 2.6 meters long; the second, 4.2 meters; the third, 1.4 meters; the fourth, 3.4 meters; and the fifth, 2.9 meters. What was the mean length of the fabric pieces Mary bought?

16. What is 0.5467 rounded to the nearest hundredth?

  (1) 0.54
  (2) 0.547
  (3) 0.55
  (4) 0.556
  (5) 0.56

17. How many deciliters is 15 milliliters?

  (1) 0.015
  (2) 0.15
  (3) 1.5
  (4) 15
  (5) 150

18. Which of the following expressions shows how to change 4.7 grams to centigrams?

  (1) 4.7×10
  (2) 4.7×100
  (3) 4.7×1000
  (4) $4.7 \div 100$
  (5) $4.7 \div 1000$

Items 19 and 20 are based on the 10-centimeter ruler shown below.

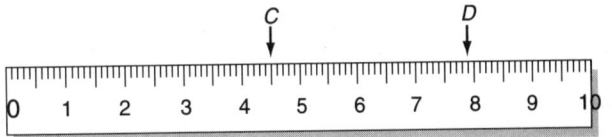

19. How many centimeters from the left end of the ruler is point *D*?

  (1) 2.1
  (2) 8.1
  (3) 7.9
  (4) 79
  (5) 81

20. What is the distance in centimeters between points *C* and *D* on the ruler?

  (1) 3.4
  (2) 3.6
  (3) 12.4
  (4) 34
  (5) 37

21. Which of the following decimals equals 0.004^3?

  (1) 0.064
  (2) 0.0064
  (3) 0.00000064
  (4) 0.000000064
  (5) 0.00000000064

22. Which of the following decimals equals $\sqrt{0.000049}$?

  (1) 0.00007
  (2) 0.0007
  (3) 0.007
  (4) 0.07
  (5) 0.7

Chapter 2, Level 2

23. What is the circumference in feet of the circle shown below?

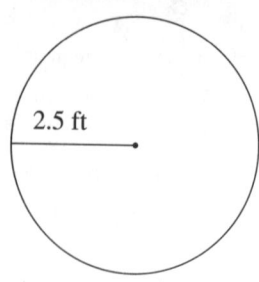

(1) 7.85
(2) 15.7
(3) 19.63
(4) 31.4
(5) 78.5

24. Which of the following expressions would show the area in square feet of the fountain shown below?

BIG PARK FOUNTAIN

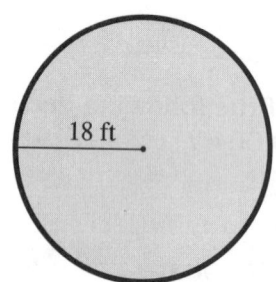

(1) 3.14×18
(2) $3.14 \times 2 \times 18$
(3) 3.14×18^2
(4) $3.14^2 \times 18$
(5) 18^2

25. What is the volume in cubic feet of the water tank shown below?

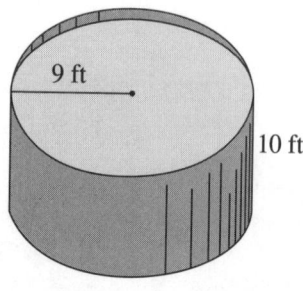

(1) 254.34
(2) 282.6
(3) 2543.4
(4) 2826
(5) 25,434

26. Which of the following expressions would show the number of meters of fencing needed to enclose the yard shown below?

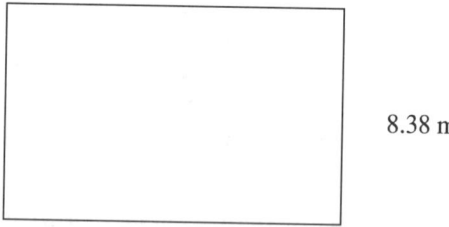

(1) $2 + 9.04 + 8.38$
(2) $2 \times 9.04 + 2 \times 8.38$
(3) $9.04 + 8.38$
(4) 9.04×8.38
(5) $9.04^2 + 8.38^2$

27. What is the area in square meters of the rectangle shown below?

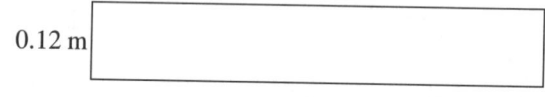

(1) 0.0024
(2) 0.024
(3) 0.24
(4) 2.4
(5) 24

28. What is the volume in cubic millimeters of the credit card shown below?

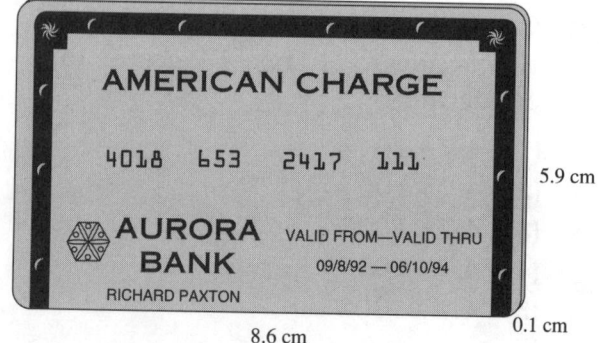

(1) 5.074
(2) 14.6
(3) 29.2
(4) 50.74
(5) 51.6

29. Ernie drove for 3.45 hours at an average speed of 57 miles per hour. Which of the following expressions would show the number of miles Ernie drove?

(1) 3.45 ÷ 57
(2) 57 + 3.45
(3) (57 + 3.45) ÷ 2
(4) 57 × 3.45
(5) 57 ÷ 3.45

30. Perry Kirk worked 31.2 hours the first week of last month, 38.5 hours the second week, 35.6 hours the third week, and 34.8 hours the fourth week. What was the median number of hours that Perry worked each week last month?

(1) 34.85
(2) 35.2
(3) 35.25
(4) 35.6
(5) 37.05

Check your answers starting on page 102.

Level 3 — Decimals Problem Solving

Items 1 to 4 are based on the following table.

WOMEN IN U.S. LABOR FORCE PER 10 FEMALES OVER 15

	1960	1970	1980	1985	1989
Rate per 10	3.6	4.1	4.8	5.1	5.4

Source: U.S. Bureau of Labor Statistics.

1. How many more women were in the labor force per 10 adult females in 1989 than in 1960?

2. Describe the change in the rate per 10 of women in the labor force from 1980 to 1989.

3. The number of adult females living in Rockville during 1989 was 25,600. If Rockville followed the national average, how many women in Rockville were in the labor force during 1989?

4. The population of Bluffton in 1989 was 52,000. The number of adult women per 10 people in Bluffton was 3.6. If Bluffton followed the national average, how many women in Bluffton were in the labor force during 1989?

Items 5 to 8 are based on the following table.

DAILY NEWSPAPER CIRCULATION (in millions)

	1970	1975	1980	1985	1988
Morning paper	25.9	25.5	29.4	36.4	40.5
Evening paper	36.2	36.2	32.8	26.4	22.2
Sunday paper	49.2	51.1	54.7	58.8	61.5

Sources: American Newspaper Publishers Association; U.S. Bureau of Census.

5. For which years were more evening papers than morning papers sold?

6. How much greater was the circulation of Sunday papers in 1988 than in 1970?

7. In what year was the circulation of Sunday papers closest to being double the circulation of morning papers?

8. The Sunday paper circulation in 1988 was how much less than the total circulation of morning and evening papers in 1988?

9. Marvin and Patricia left a restaurant at the same time and drove in the same direction. If Marvin drove at 40 miles per hour and Patricia drove at 50 miles per hour, how many miles apart were they after 0.75 of an hour?

10. Two trains left Chicago at the same time. One headed east for New York; the other headed west for Denver. If they were both traveling at 56 miles per hour, how many miles apart were they after 3.5 hours?

11. John and Brett left their house at the same time. John went south and Brett went north. Brett drove at 50 miles per hour. John drove at 55 miles per hour. How many miles apart were they after 4.25 hours?

12. Sue earns $5.50 an hour for the first 40 hours she works each week. She earns $8.25 an hour for working overtime. How much would she earn if she worked 45 hours in one week?

13. The tripmeter in Dave's car read 312.5 miles since he last filled the gas tank. He refilled the tank with 9.6 gallons of gas. To the nearest mile, what is the average distance that he drove on one gallon of gas?

14. Marcia bought a 10.8-pound turkey for $4.86. What was the price per pound of the turkey?

15. The average rainfall for July and August in Platteville is 10.8 inches. This July it rained 7.9 inches, and this August, 8.5 inches. How much above or below the average was the rainfall for this July and August?

16. Morton had five packages to mail.

    Package A weighed 2.05 kg.
    Package B weighed 0.25 kg.
    Package C weighed 2.5 kg.
    Package D weighed 2.15 kg.
    Package E weighed 0.55 kg.

    Arrange these packages in order from lightest to heaviest.

Items 17 to 20 cannot be answered due to insufficient data. Tell what information is needed to answer the question in each item.

17. Doug caught four fish. The heaviest weighed 6.3 pounds and the lightest weighed 1.8 pounds. What was the average weight of the fish he caught?

18. Peter bought a 5-pound package of ground beef for $9.45 and a T-bone steak for $5.80. How much more per pound was the steak than the ground beef?

19. Bruce bought carpet for his living room that cost $15 a yard. His living room is 8 yards wide. What was the total cost of the carpet?

20. According to the table about newspaper circulation for Items 5 to 8, how many more people had the morning paper delivered than the evening paper delivered in 1988?

Items 21 to 24 are based on the following table.

BIRTH RATE PER 1000 PEOPLE IN UNITED STATES

	1960	1965	1970	1975	1980	1985	1990
Rate per 1000	23.7	19.4	18.4	14.8	15.9	15.8	16.7

Source: Department of Health and Human Services.

21. How does the birth rate per 1000 in 1990 compare to the birth rate in 1960?

   (1) 0.9 more
   (2) 7.0 less
   (3) 7.0 more
   (4) 7.7 less
   (5) 40.4 more

22. The population of Fountaintown in 1990 was 34,000. If Fountaintown followed the national average, how many babies were born in Fountaintown during 1990?

   (1) 17
   (2) 51
   (3) 568
   (4) 2036
   (5) 567,800

23. The population of Bridgeton was 19,000 in 1980 and 23,000 in 1990. If Bridgeton follows the national average, how many more babies were born in Bridgeton in 1990 than in 1980?

   (1) 15
   (2) 18
   (3) 67
   (4) 82
   (5) 84

24. Which of the following expresses the pattern for the birth rate per 1000 for the years shown in the table?

   (1) The rate remained steady.
   (2) The rate increased.
   (3) The rate decreased.
   (4) The rate increased and then gradually decreased.
   (5) The rate decreased and then gradually increased.

Items 25 to 28 are based on the following table.

Car	Miles per Gallon	Tank Size (in gallons)
Rhino	4.3	30
Hippo	8.8	25
Camel	12.2	25
Antelope	21.7	15
Carp	38.5	10

25. How many miles can the Rhino travel on a full tank of gas?

   (1) 12
   (2) 43
   (3) 86
   (4) 107
   (5) 129

26. If a Hippo traveled 184.8 miles, how many gallons of gasoline did it use?

   (1) 18
   (2) 20
   (3) 21
   (4) 23
   (5) 25

27. If gasoline costs $1.189 per gallon and the tank of the Camel has 7.2 gallons in it, how much will it cost to fill the tank?

   (1) $ 5.95
   (2) $ 8.56
   (3) $20.16
   (4) $21.16
   (5) $29.73

28. Which expression shows how many miles farther than an Antelope a Carp can travel on a full tank of gas?

Chapter 3: Fractions

Level 1: Fractions Skills

1. Reduce $\frac{8}{20}$ to lowest terms.

2. Raise $\frac{7}{16}$ to 96ths.

3. Change $\frac{62}{12}$ to a mixed number in lowest terms.

4. Change $4\frac{4}{13}$ to an improper fraction.

5. Add $\frac{5}{6}$ and $\frac{7}{12}$.

6. Which is larger, $\frac{5}{8}$ or $\frac{7}{12}$?

7. Subtract $1\frac{8}{9}$ from 6.

8. Multiply $\frac{7}{9} \times \frac{3}{8} \times \frac{5}{14}$.

9. Change 0.075 to a fraction and reduce.

10. What is $15 \div 1\frac{1}{5}$?

11. Multiply $\frac{5}{8}$ by 6.

12. Arrange the following fractions in order from largest to smallest: $\frac{4}{9}, \frac{5}{6}, \frac{5}{12}, \frac{7}{18}$.

13. Change 7.8 to a mixed number and reduce.

14. Change $\frac{6}{25}$ to a decimal.

15. Subtract $2\frac{5}{8}$ from $5\frac{1}{2}$.

16. Add $5\frac{1}{4}$, $1\frac{2}{3}$, and $\frac{5}{6}$.

17. Find the difference between $2\frac{1}{3}$ and $4\frac{2}{5}$.

18. Multiply $1\frac{3}{5} \times 4\frac{1}{6}$.

19. Divide $\frac{8}{21}$ by $\frac{4}{7}$.

20. Find the quotient of $1\frac{1}{2}$ divided by $2\frac{3}{4}$.

Check your answers starting on page 105.

Level 2: Fractions Application

1. Of the 81 employees at the Widget Co., 59 work in the factory. What fraction of the employees work in the factory?

2. What part of a ton is 500 pounds?

3. Change 164 minutes to hours and minutes.

4. Change 6 quarts to pints.

Items 5 and 6 are based on the ruler shown below.

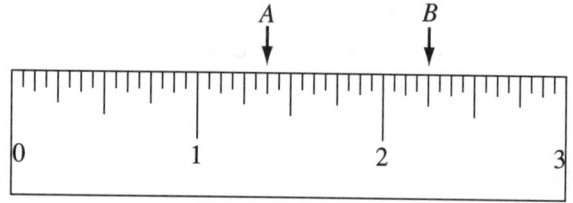

5. How far from the left end of the ruler is point *A*?

6. What is the distance between points *A* and *B*?

7. Find the value of $\left(\frac{3}{20}\right)^2$.

8. What is the square root of $\frac{121}{169}$?

9. What is the area of the figure shown below?

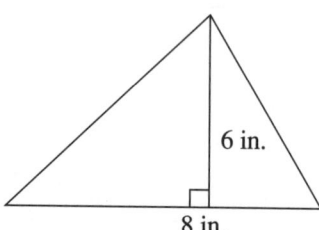

10. What is the perimeter in feet of the figure shown below?

11. What is the area of a parallelogram with a base of 6 feet and a height of $1\frac{3}{4}$ feet?

12. Julie bought a coat on sale for $80. This coat is regularly priced at $130. What is the ratio of the sale price to the regular price?

13. If 4:7 = 52:*t*, what does *t* equal?

14. Amanda Young purchased three raffle tickets. If 1800 tickets were sold for one prize, what is the probability that she will win?

15. Mike had four apples, five bananas, two pears, and three oranges in a bowl. If his son grabbed an orange, what is the probability that the next piece of fruit a person grabs will be a banana?

16. During a flu epidemic, 27 out of 72 employees were sick. What fraction of employees were not sick?

    (1) $\frac{3}{8}$

Chapter 3: Fractions

(2) $\frac{5}{8}$
(3) $\frac{2}{5}$
(4) $\frac{3}{5}$
(5) Insufficient data is given to solve the problem.

17. How many yards does $4\frac{1}{2}$ feet equal?
   (1) $\frac{3}{8}$
   (2) $\frac{2}{3}$
   (3) 1
   (4) $1\frac{1}{2}$
   (5) $13\frac{1}{2}$

18. How many seconds are in $1\frac{1}{2}$ minutes?
   (1) 30
   (2) 40
   (3) 45
   (4) $60\frac{1}{2}$
   (5) 90

19. How many gallons do 14 quarts equal?
   (1) $3\frac{1}{2}$
   (2) 4
   (3) 7
   (4) 28
   (5) 56

Items 20 and 21 are based on the ruler shown below.

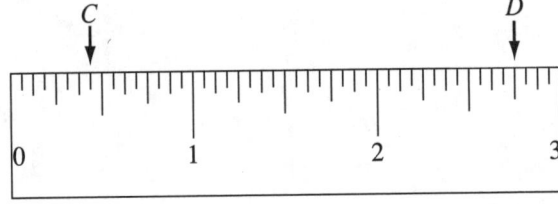

20. How many inches from the left end of the ruler is point D?
   (1) $\frac{1}{4}$
   (2) $\frac{7}{8}$

(3) $2\frac{3}{4}$
(4) $2\frac{6}{4}$
(5) $3\frac{1}{4}$

21. What is the distance in inches between points C and D?
   (1) $1\frac{7}{8}$
   (2) $2\frac{1}{4}$
   (3) $2\frac{5}{16}$
   (4) $2\frac{3}{4}$
   (5) $3\frac{3}{16}$

22. What does $\left(\frac{2}{5}\right)^3$ equal?
   (1) $\frac{8}{125}$
   (2) $\frac{6}{15}$
   (3) $\frac{5}{8}$
   (4) 1
   (5) $1\frac{1}{5}$

23. What is the square root of $\frac{4}{9}$?

24. What is the perimeter in inches of the square computer disk shown below?

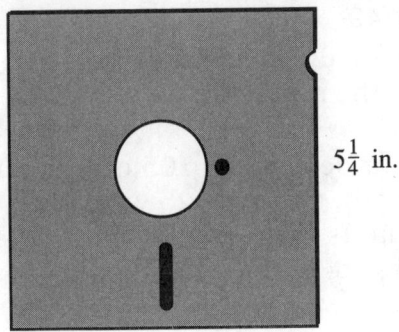

   (1) 6
   (2) $10\frac{1}{2}$
   (3) 21
   (4) $27\frac{9}{16}$
   (5) Insufficient data is given to solve the problem.

Chapter 3, Level 2

25. What is the area in square feet of the triangle shown below?

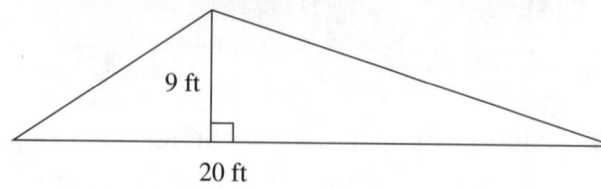

- (1) $14\frac{1}{2}$
- (2) 45
- (3) 90
- (4) 180
- (5) Insufficient data is given to solve the problem.

26. What is the area in square inches of the parallelogram shown below?

- (1) 7
- (2) 28
- (3) 35
- (4) 49
- (5) Insufficient data is given to solve the problem.

27. A car dealer sold 105 cars in one month. Of these, 25 were used cars. What is the ratio of used cars to new cars sold?

- (1) $\frac{5}{21}$
- (2) $\frac{16}{21}$
- (3) $\frac{5}{16}$
- (4) $\frac{16}{5}$
- (5) Insufficient data is given to solve the problem.

28. If $\frac{3}{10} = \frac{b}{30}$, what does b equal?

- (1) 1
- (2) $3\frac{1}{3}$
- (3) 9
- (4) 90
- (5) 100

29. A raffle offers six prizes. If 3900 tickets have been sold, what is the probability that a ticket will be worth a prize?

- (1) $\frac{1}{390}$
- (2) $\frac{1}{600}$
- (3) $\frac{1}{650}$
- (4) $\frac{1}{660}$
- (5) $\frac{1}{3900}$

30. There were six sweatshirts, ten sweatpants, eight T-shirts, and three sweaters left on the sale table in a store. What is the probability that the next customer will grab a sweatshirt or sweatpants?

- (1) $\frac{16}{9}$
- (2) $\frac{2}{27}$
- (3) $\frac{6}{27}$
- (4) $\frac{10}{27}$
- (5) $\frac{16}{27}$

Check your answers starting on page 105.

Chapter 3: Fractions

Level 3: Fractions Problem Solving

1. The ratio of peanuts to cashews in a mixture of nuts is 5:2. How many pounds of cashews need to be mixed with 15 pounds of peanuts?

2. Darwin earned $45.60 by working 6 hours. How much will he make working a 40-hour week?

3. The ratio of salaried to non-salaried employees at Webber Manufacturing is 2:25. If there are 375 non-salaried employees at this company, how many salaried employees are there?

4. Ginny used 12 gallons of gas to travel 336 miles. If she continues to get the same fuel efficiency, how far can she travel on 20 gallons?

5. The scale on a map is $\frac{1}{4}$ inch = 20 miles. Two cities are 140 miles apart. How far apart will they appear on this map?

6. The ratio of hamburgers to chicken sandwiches sold at a fast-food restaurant is 7:3. If a total of 430 hamburgers and sandwiches were sold, how many of those were chicken sandwiches.

7. The ratio of telephone calls made to telephone calls received is 2:11. If the telephone was used a total of 338 times in one month, how many calls were received?

8. In a recent survey 8 out of 11 people said they watched television at least once a week. If 1430 people were polled, how many said they did not watch television?

9. Out of every 10 employees at the Blumford Company, one is a manager. If 648 people are not managers, how many people are employed there?

10. The ratio of adults to children at an apartment complex is 9:8. If there are 187 people living in the complex, how many are adults?

11. A restaurant sells $\frac{1}{4}$-pound hamburgers for $2.25 each. In one week, 626 pounds of hamburger were sold. How many hamburgers were sold that week?

12. Janet Cooke caught a fish weighing $3\frac{1}{8}$ pounds, Robert Cuquire caught a fish weighing $3\frac{7}{8}$ pounds, and Chris Wastle caught a fish weighing $2\frac{9}{16}$ pounds. How many pounds more did Janet's fish weigh than Chris's?

13. Jack Brattel has four boards each measuring $10\frac{1}{8}$ feet in length and three boards each measuring $8\frac{1}{2}$ feet in length. If he takes one of the longer boards and cuts it into nine equal pieces, how many feet will each piece measure?

14. Natalie Nasher's extended family has a total of 57 people in it, including 9 nephews and 15 nieces. What is the ratio of nieces to nephews?

15. Jeanette just bought a bookcase that is $4\frac{1}{2}$ feet long, $1\frac{1}{2}$ feet deep, and 6 feet high. How much area of the floor will this cover?

Chapter 3, Level 3

(1) $\dfrac{(2 \times \$730)}{5}$

(2) $\dfrac{(2 \times \$730)}{7}$

(3) $\dfrac{(3 \times \$730)}{5}$

(4) $\dfrac{(5 \times \$730)}{2}$

(5) $\dfrac{(5 \times \$730)}{3}$

35. A triangle with a perimeter of 12 feet has a base of 4 feet and a height of 3 feet. What is the area of this triangle in square feet?

(1) 6
(2) 12
(3) 18
(4) 24
(5) 72

36. Henry has $5\frac{3}{4}$ pounds of apples. If he shares them among four persons, which of the following expressions would show how much each person would receive?

(1) $5\frac{3}{4} \div 4$
(2) $5\frac{3}{4} \div \frac{1}{4}$
(3) $5\frac{3}{4} - 4$
(4) $5\frac{3}{4} + 4$
(5) $5\frac{3}{4} + \frac{1}{4}$

37. Barbara Jones drove 207 miles on $6\frac{9}{10}$ gallons of gas. What was her car's fuel efficiency in miles per gallon?

(1) 19
(2) 30
(3) 35
(4) 143
(5) Insufficient data is given to solve the problem.

38. Ralph Mooseman spends $\frac{3}{5}$ of his time at work making sales calls. How many hours did he spend making sales calls last week?

(1) 3
(2) 5
(3) 21
(4) 24
(5) Insufficient data is given to solve the problem.

39. What is the correct order of the following spices from smallest to largest by weight?

Spice	Weight (in ounces)
A. Cloves	$\frac{7}{24}$
B. Ginger	$\frac{1}{6}$
C. Rosemary	$\frac{3}{16}$
D. Sage	$\frac{5}{8}$
E. Thyme	$\frac{5}{12}$

(1) A, D, E, C, B
(2) B, C, A, E, D
(3) C, B, A, D, E
(4) D, C, A, B, E
(5) E, D, C, B, A

40. Mary Quernia made $9\frac{1}{2}$ quarts of tomato sauce using the vegetables from her garden. Which of the following expresses how many pints this is?

(1) $\frac{1}{2} \div 9\frac{1}{2}$
(2) $2 \div 9\frac{1}{2}$
(3) $9\frac{1}{2} \times \frac{1}{2}$
(4) $9\frac{1}{2} \times 2$
(5) $9\frac{1}{2} \div 2$

Check your answers starting on page 106.

28 Chapter 3: Fractions

Chapter 4: Percents

Level 1: Percents Skills

1. Change 0.82 to a percent.

2. Change 73% to a decimal.

3. Change 64% to a fraction reduced to lowest terms.

4. Change $\frac{11}{20}$ to a percent

5. Change $\frac{1}{11}$ to a percent.

6. Change 41.5% to a fraction reduced to lowest terms.

7. Change 0.00125 to a percent.

8. Change 0.072% to a decimal.

9. Change $5\frac{5}{8}$% to a fraction reduced to lowest terms.

10. Find 75% of 15.

11. Find 0.2% of 20.

12. 30 is what percent of 150?

13. 55 is what percent of 20?

14. 18 is what percent of 48?

15. 27 is 60% of what number?

16. $66\frac{2}{3}$% of what number is 64?

17. 3% of what number is 9?

Complete the following table.

	Fraction	Decimal	Percent
18.			$33\frac{1}{3}$%
19.	$\frac{5}{6}$		
20.			$12\frac{1}{2}$%

Check your answers starting on page 108.

Level 2: Percents Application

1. Thomas bought a suit at a clearance sale for 50% off the regular price. If the suit originally cost $170, how much did he save?

2. A movie theater has 540 seats. If at a recent showing the theater was 35% full, how many seats were occupied?

3. Sylvia earns $1398 a month. She puts $12\frac{1}{2}\%$ of her salary into a savings account. How much does she deposit every month?

4. According to a recent census, in a town of 34,640 people, 2.5% of the people said they did not like flying in airplanes. How many people in this town liked flying?

5. The Fighting Canaries won 18 out of 25 games. What percent did they win?

6. For a meal that cost $12.50, Raul paid sales tax of $0.75. The sales tax was what percent of the cost?

7. During an outbreak of the flu, 120 out of 360 employees at a factory were sick. What percent of the employees were sick?

8. Rudolph earns $1600 per month. A total of $328 is deducted from his pay. What percent of his earnings is deducted?

9. On a test Myron got 21 questions correct for a score of 75%. What was the total number of questions on the test?

10. Jack saved $35 on a new coat. This is 20% of the original price. Find the original price.

11. The Smythes paid $11,070 in taxes last year. That was 27% of their total earnings. What were their total earnings?

12. During a recent charity drive 114 people agreed to make a donation. This was $66\frac{2}{3}\%$ of the people contacted in a certain area. How many people were contacted?

For items 13 to 15, find the interest.

13. $140 at 7% annual interest for 3 years

14. $1500 at 12% annual interest for 6 months

15. $90 at $4\frac{1}{2}\%$ annual interest for 1 year

16. Regina purchased a new car for $8500. She made a down payment of 20%. Which of the following amounts was her down payment?

    (1) $ 650
    (2) $ 850
    (3) $1700
    (4) $4250
    (5) Insufficient data is given to solve the problem.

17. Grant bought a book that cost $11.50. He had to pay a 5% sales tax. How much was the tax?

    (1) $0.23
    (2) $0.57

30 Chapter 4: Percents

(3) $0.58
(4) $1.15
(5) $2.30

18. Pedro earned $7.20 per hour. He was given a 6.25% raise. Which of the following expressions would show the amount of his raise?

(1) 0.0625 × $7.20
(2) 0.625 × $7.20
(3) $7.20 ÷ 0.0625
(4) $7.20 × 6.25
(5) $7.20 + 6.25

19. When Mary and Marty sold their house, it was worth 35% more than what they paid for it. If they bought it for $55,000, how much more was it worth when they sold it?

(1) $19,250
(2) $20,000
(3) $28,571
(4) $74,250
(5) $90,000

20. During the softball season Reggie Mays got hits 34 times out of 136 times at bat. What percent of the time did he get a hit?

(1) 12%
(2) 25%
(3) 33%
(4) 40%
(5) 98%

21. Sally works on an inspection line. In one shift 6 out of 480 products were found to be defective. What percent were defective?

(1) $\frac{3}{4}$%
(2) $1\frac{1}{4}$%
(3) $2\frac{1}{2}$%
(4) $3\frac{3}{4}$%
(5) $7\frac{1}{2}$%

22. Wilbur took a spelling test and spelled 105 words correctly. What percent did he get right?

(1) 15%
(2) $23\frac{1}{2}$%
(3) $64\frac{1}{2}$%
(4) 75%
(5) Insufficient data is given to solve the problem.

23. Out of 21 meals per week, Debra eats 5 of them in restaurants. Which of the following would show the percent of the time she eats out?

(1) $\frac{21 \times 100}{5}$
(2) $\frac{5 \times 100}{21}$
(3) $\frac{5 \times 21}{100}$
(4) $\frac{21}{5 \times 100}$
(5) $\frac{5}{21 \times 100}$

24. Norman was at work 95% of the time over a 1-year period. If he worked 247 days, how many days in all could he have worked?

(1) 230
(2) 250
(3) 255
(4) 260
(5) 275

25. Otto paid $189.23 in sales tax for a new motorcycle. If the tax rate was 5%, how much did the motorcycle cost?

(1) $1892.60
(2) $2555.60
(3) $2944.60
(4) $3157.60
(5) $3784.60

26. On the first day of her bicycle trip,

Chapter 4, Level 2

Karen rode 80 miles, which was 2.5% of the distance she planned to ride. How many miles was she planning to ride?

(1) 200
(2) 320
(3) 2000
(4) 3200
(5) 20,000

27. A hospital has 51 patients, which is 34% of its total capacity. Which expression would show the hospital's total capacity?

(1) $0.34 \div 51$
(2) $\dfrac{34 \times 100}{51}$
(3) $\dfrac{51 \times 34}{100}$
(4) 51×0.34
(5) $51 \div 0.34$

28. Velma deposited $230 in her bank at 6% interest for 2 years. How much interest did she earn?

(1) $14.50
(2) $21.30
(3) $27.60
(4) $39.80
(5) $46.00

29. If Quentin borrows $1385 for 3 years and 3 months, how much interest will he pay?

(1) $221.60
(2) $240.20
(3) $328.85
(4) $360.10
(5) Insufficient data is given to solve the problem.

30. Brett borrowed $172 for 8 months at 15% simple interest. Which of the following expressions would show how much interest he will have to pay?

(1) $\dfrac{\$172}{1} \times \dfrac{15}{1} \times \dfrac{2}{3}$
(2) $\dfrac{\$172}{1} \times \dfrac{15}{1} \times \dfrac{3}{4}$
(3) $\dfrac{\$172}{1} \times \dfrac{15}{100} \times \dfrac{1}{8}$
(4) $\dfrac{\$172}{1} \times \dfrac{15}{100} \times \dfrac{2}{3}$
(5) $\dfrac{\$172}{1} \times \dfrac{15}{100} \times \dfrac{8}{1}$

Check your answers starting on page 109.

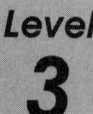

Level 3 — Percents Problem Solving

1. Hubert invested $450 in the stock market. After a year, his investment had increased by 12%. What was the value of his investment after a year?

2. A set of tires regularly priced at $270 was on sale for $33\frac{1}{3}\%$ off. Find the sale price of the tires.

3. Marsha bought shoes for $42 and a purse for $28. She had to pay sales tax of 7%. What was the total cost of her purchases, including tax?

4. Manny bought a television set for $240, reduced from $320. Find the discount rate (percent of decrease).

5. Belinda spent $24 for food and $96 for lodging on a recent business trip. What percent of her expenses went for lodging?

6. A dealer reduced the price of a new car by $1485. If the sticker price was $9900, what percent of the sticker price was the reduced price?

7. Louis buys cans of soup for his grocery for $0.30 each and sells them for $0.48 each. By what percent does he mark up the price?

8. Ramona rides the bus 12 miles to get to work. This is 96% of the distance from her house to her job. How many miles is it from her house to the bus stop?

9. Peter rents an apartment for $456 a month. This is 30% of his monthly take-home pay. How much money does he have for other expenses?

10. Frank has saved $6560. This is 82% of the amount he needs for a down payment on a house. How much more does he need?

11. During a recent election, a candidate for the state Senate won 77 precincts. This was 87.5% of the precincts in the district. How many precincts did she lose?

12. Kent received a 12.5% raise from his hourly rate of $9.20. Blake received a raise of $0.98 an hour. How much more was Kent's raise than Blake's?

13. Leonard earns a weekly salary of $40 plus a commission of 25% of his sales. Sharon is paid a salary of $772 every two weeks. If Leonard's sales total $1604 for one week, how much more than Sharon will he make?

14. Valerie earns $1260 a month. She spends 30% of that on groceries. Another $415 is spent for housing. How much more does she spend for housing than for groceries?

15. Patricia is shopping for a new car. One dealer is willing to give her a 16% discount on the sticker price of $9899. Another dealer will discount the price of the same model by $1495. How much more will Patricia save by buying the car from the first dealer?

Items 16 to 20 are based on the following information.

Income tax rates are based on the amount of income a person makes. Generally, the tax rate is higher for people with higher incomes.

The tax is based on the net income of an individual or family. The net is found by combining all forms of income, such as wages, tips, rents, dividends, and interest, and subtracting from that total various deductible expenses, such as medical care, depreciation, contributions, some loan interest, and other taxes paid.

Once a net income is found, the tax is figured by looking at tax tables. Generally, the table gives an income figure, the tax for that amount, and the tax rate for the amount over that.

16. Harold's net income is $17,576. How much will his taxes be at a rate of 15%?

17. Erica earned $21,098 from wages and $347 in dividends. Her deductions totaled $5884. At a tax rate of 15%, what will her taxes be?

18. Theresa uses her computer in her business and is able to depreciate part of its value every year. If the

computer is valued at $2564, and she deducts $512.80 of it for depreciation, what percent of the computer's value has she deducted?

19. Gertrude's new income totaled $29,000. The tax tables state that her taxes are $4095 plus 28% of the amount of income over $27,300. What are Gertrude's total taxes?

20. Marie and Ivan earned $45,765 and are able to deduct $3986 for medical expenses, $2539 for loan interest, and $400 for contributions. The tax tables state that their taxes are $5100 plus 28% of the amount of income over $34,000. What are their total taxes?

21. Carol weighed 175 pounds last year. During the past year, she lost 32% of her weight. How many pounds does she weigh now?

(1) 56
(2) 119
(3) 143
(4) 207
(5) 231

22. Gasoline at Josh's Interstate Tourist Service is 40% higher than at Howard's Downtown Service. If gas at Howard's is priced at $1.20, what is the price at Josh's?

(1) $0.48
(2) $0.72
(3) $1.60
(4) $1.68
(5) Insufficient data is given to solve the problem.

23. Pamela selected a ring for her husband priced at $420. She made a down payment of 25%. Which expression would show how much she still needs to pay?

(1) $\frac{1}{4} \times \$420$
(2) $\$420 + \$25$
(3) $\$420 - \$25$
(4) $\$420 + \left(\frac{1}{4} \times \$420\right)$
(5) $\$420 - \left(\frac{1}{4} \times \$420\right)$

24. Jill paid $40 for a certain type of sweater she sells in her shop. If she puts a 90% markup on these sweaters, how much does she charge for each sweater?

(1) $ 36
(2) $ 50
(3) $ 76
(4) $ 90
(5) $130

25. Sherman paid $9500 for his car when he bought it new. He was given $5700 for it when he traded it in. By what percent had his car depreciated?

(1) 40%
(2) 45%
(3) 50%
(4) 55%
(5) 60%

26. Albert purchased a share of stock for $86. He sold it for $73.10. Which of the following expresses the percent by which the price dropped?

(1) $\dfrac{\$86 + \$73.10}{\$73.10} \times 100$

(2) $\dfrac{\$86 - \$73.10}{\$73.10} \times 100$

(3) $\dfrac{\$86 + \$73.10}{\$86} \times 100$

(4) $\dfrac{\$86 - \$73.10}{\$86} \times 100$

(5) $\dfrac{\$73.10}{\$86 - \$73.10} \times 100$

27. The population of Coalville in 1980 increased to 5368 in 1990. By what percent did it increase?

(1) 9%
(2) 15%
(3) 22%
(4) 28%
(5) Insufficient data is given to solve the problem.

28. Ramon has 45 college credit hours. This is 37.5% of the amount he needs to earn a degree. How many more hours does he need?

(1) 45
(2) 75
(3) 95
(4) 105
(5) 120

29. Warren bought a microwave oven on sale for $165. This is 80% of the list price. How much did Warren save by buying the oven on sale?

(1) $ 33
(2) $ 41.25
(3) $ 85
(4) $132
(5) $206.25

30. After using a new hybrid seed, Frank's yield of corn increased by 2 bushels per acre. This is an increase of 5% over his previous corn yield. How many bushels per acre is Frank's new yield?

(1) 35
(2) 38
(3) 42
(4) 45
(5) Insufficient data is given to solve the problem.

31. Sandra's business expenses totaled $294,912, which was 72% of the business's gross sales. Which expression would show her business's net sales?

(1) $\$294{,}912 + \dfrac{\$294{,}912}{0.72}$

(2) $\$294{,}912 - \dfrac{\$294{,}912}{0.72}$

(3) $\$294{,}912 \times 0.72 + \$294{,}912$

(4) $\dfrac{\$294{,}912}{0.72} + \$294{,}912$

(5) $\dfrac{\$294{,}912}{0.72} - \$294{,}912$

32. Which of the following sales taxes will be the highest?

(1) 5% on a purchase of $1.00
(2) 3% on a purchase of $1.75
(3) 7% on a purchase of $0.95
(4) 4% on a purchase of $1.50
(5) 2% on a purchase of $2.50

33. Tamara has five choices for future employment. Which of the following options will provide her the best annual income?

(1) Keeping her present job at $15,000 per year plus a 20% year-end bonus
(2) Taking a job that pays $1250 per month
(3) Taking a sales job that pays 3% commission with guaranteed sales of at least $150,000
(4) Taking a job that pays $420 per week
(5) Taking a job that pays $18,600 per year

34. Which of the following items was the Rambons' largest expense?

(1) A property tax bill of $984
(2) Local income taxes on $29,500 at a tax rate of 4%
(3) Twelve loan payments of $129 each
(4) A down payment of 12% on a new car costing $10,800

Chapter 4, Level 3   35

(5) Insurance payments as follows: medical, $750; auto, $598; and life, $621

35. Which of the following salespersons had the least earnings?

   (1) Frank gets an 8% commission on sales of $4000 plus a salary of $150.
   (2) Bernice gets a 10% commission on sales of $4900.
   (3) Roger gets a 20% commission on sales of $2000 and a 25% commission on sales of $300.
   (4) Holly gets a 20% commission on sales of $3000.
   (5) Natalie gets a 40% commission on sales of $1400.

Items 36 to 40 are based on the following information.

Every 10 years the government takes a census in which it counts the number of people living in the United States. The census shows, among other things, what parts of the country are growing in population and by how much. The census also provides the government with a certain amount of information about people, such as how many telephones they own.

Most important, perhaps, the census is used to determine the boundaries of the districts of representatives to the U.S. Congress. Each district sends one representative to Congress. As the population of districts change, so do the districts.

36. Boombuston's population grew from the last census by 38%. If its population was 9800 people, what is its current population?

   (1) 13,524
   (2) 15,734
   (3) 16,864
   (4) 18,936
   (5) Insufficient data is given to solve the problem.

37. One state's population totaled 6,326,000. If every 2% of the population sends a representative to the state legislature, how many people will one person represent?

   (1) 12,652
   (2) 61,994
   (3) 126,520
   (4) 619,948
   (5) 1,265,200

38. The census found that the number of homes with two or more telephones in Sweetring County increased by 374, an increase of 5%. Now how many homes have two or more telephones?

   (1) 3740
   (2) 4480
   (3) 6675
   (4) 6986
   (5) 7854

39. Townesty County's population dropped from 40,000 to 35,000. By what percent did it decrease?

   (1) 5%
   (2) $12\frac{1}{2}\%$
   (3) $14\frac{2}{7}\%$
   (4) $46\frac{2}{3}\%$
   (5) 50%

40. The City of Albatron grew by 6% from a population of 356,000. Cattleville's population increased by 78,000 people from a population of 350,000. How many more people now live in Cattleville than in Albatron?

   (1) 12,810
   (2) 21,360
   (3) 42,800
   (4) 50,640
   (5) 56,640

Check your answers starting on page 111.

Chapter 4: Percents

Chapter 5: Graphs

Items 1 to 7 are based on the pictograph shown below.

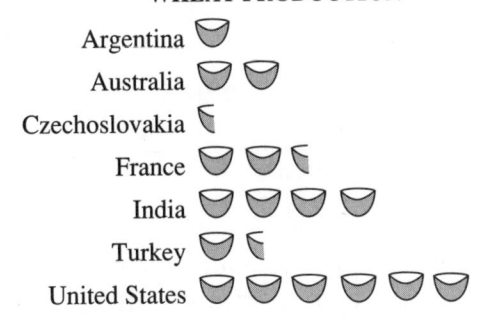

WHEAT PRODUCTION

Argentina 🥣
Australia 🥣🥣
Czechoslovakia 🥣
France 🥣🥣🥣
India 🥣🥣🥣🥣
Turkey 🥣🥣
United States 🥣🥣🥣🥣🥣

LEGEND:
Each 🥣 = 10,000 metric tons

1. How many metric tons of wheat did Australia produce?

2. Which country produced the most wheat?

3. France produced how many times more wheat than Czechoslovakia?

4. How many more metric tons of wheat than India did the United States produce?

5. If 20% of the wheat grown in the United States is exported, how many metric tons is that?

6. If wheat is worth $129 per metric ton, what would be the value of the wheat grown in Turkey?

7. If total world production of wheat is 490,000 metric tons, how many bushel baskets would be needed to show that amount?

Items 8 to 13 are based on the circle graph below showing how a certain service organization spends each dollar it raises.

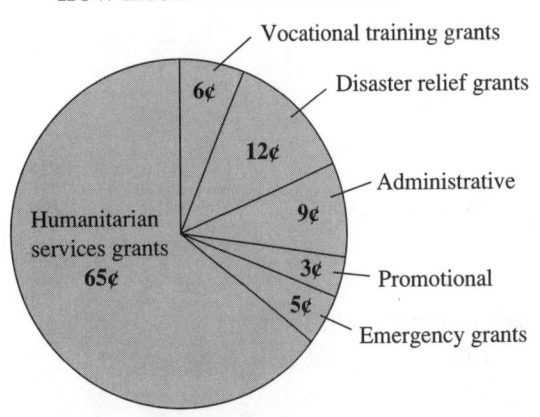

HOW EACH DOLLAR IS SPENT

- Vocational training grants: 6¢
- Disaster relief grants: 12¢
- Administrative: 9¢
- Promotional: 3¢
- Emergency grants: 5¢
- Humanitarian services grants: 65¢

8. What percent of the organization's expenses went to emergency grants?

9. Which category shown on the graph represents the smallest expenditure by the organization?

10. What fraction in lowest terms of the organization's total expenditures is used for disaster relief grants?

11. Together, which two categories make up approximately one-fifth of the organization's total expenditures?

12. If this organization raised $2 million, how much did it spend for humanitarian service grants?

13. If this organization raised $2 million, how many more dollars did it spend for vocational grants than for emergency grants?

Items 14 to 19 are based on the bar graph shown below.

AVERAGE WEEKLY EARNINGS

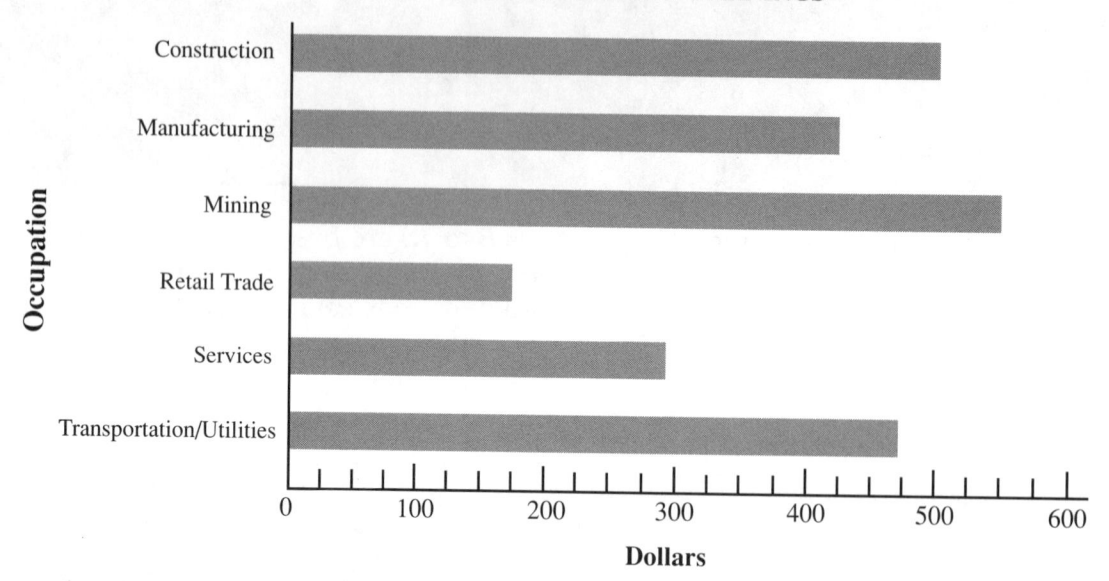

14. Which category had the highest-paying salary?

15. Which occupation had an average weekly salary of $290?

16. The salary of which occupation is approximately equal to the salary of construction workers?

17. What is the difference between the average weekly earnings of a retail trade employee and a manufacturing employee?

18. What would be the average annual salary for a transportation/utility employee?

19. For a 40-hour workweek, what is the average hourly earnings of a mining employee?

Items 20 to 23 are based on the divided bar graph shown below.

HIGHEST AND LOWEST ALTITUDES OF SELECTED STATES

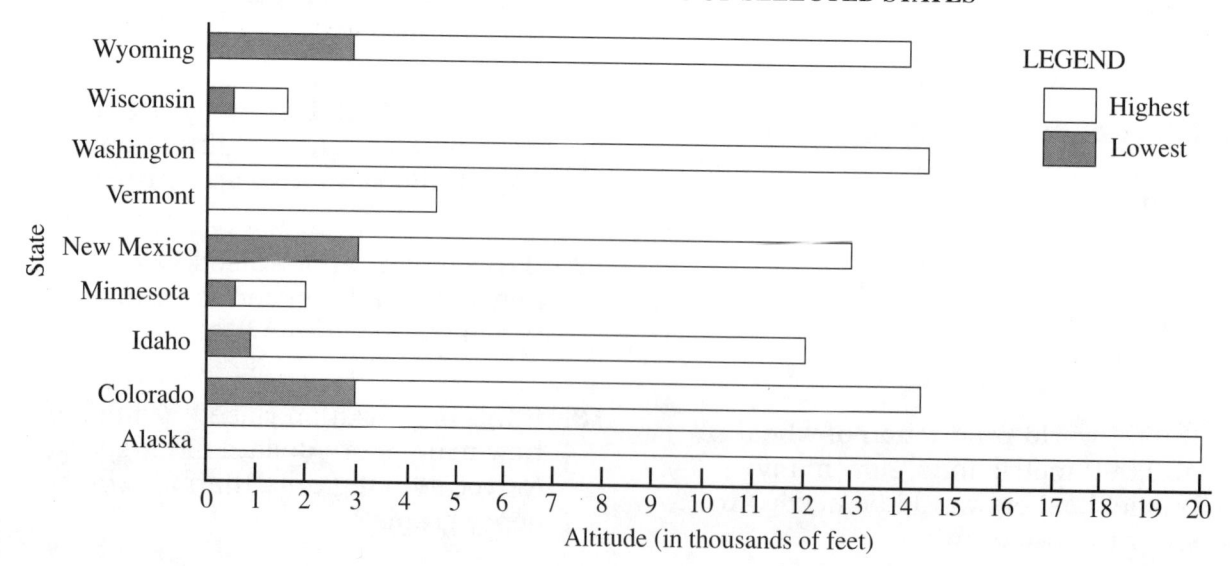

38   Chapter 5: Graphs

20. Which states have a lowest altitude of sea level (zero feet)?

21. Which state has the lowest highest altitude?

22. What is the approximate difference in feet between the highest and lowest points in Idaho?

23. Approximately how many times higher than the highest point in Minnesota is the highest point in Wyoming?

Items 24 to 30 are based on the line graph shown below.

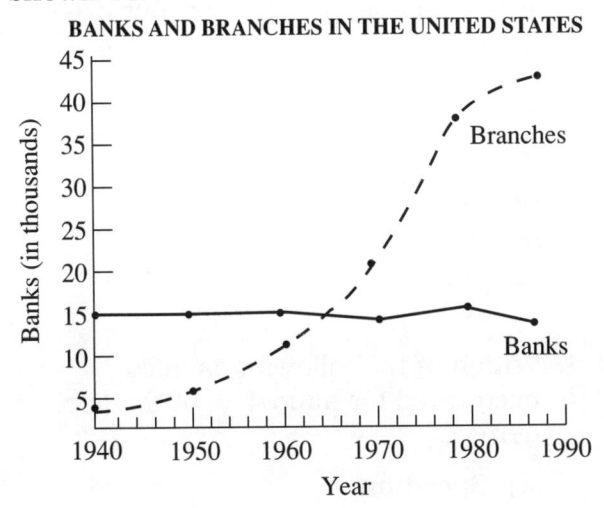

BANKS AND BRANCHES IN THE UNITED STATES

24. In what year did the number of bank branches reach 5000?

25. After what year did the number of banks first show an increase?

26. In what year were the number of banks and the number of branches equal?

27. How many banks were there in 1940?

28. In 1970, approximately how many branches were there?

29. Approximately how many more branches than banks were there in 1980?

30. In which decade did the number of branches show the greatest increase?

Items 31 to 36 are based on the pictograph shown below.

WORLD SERIES RECORDS

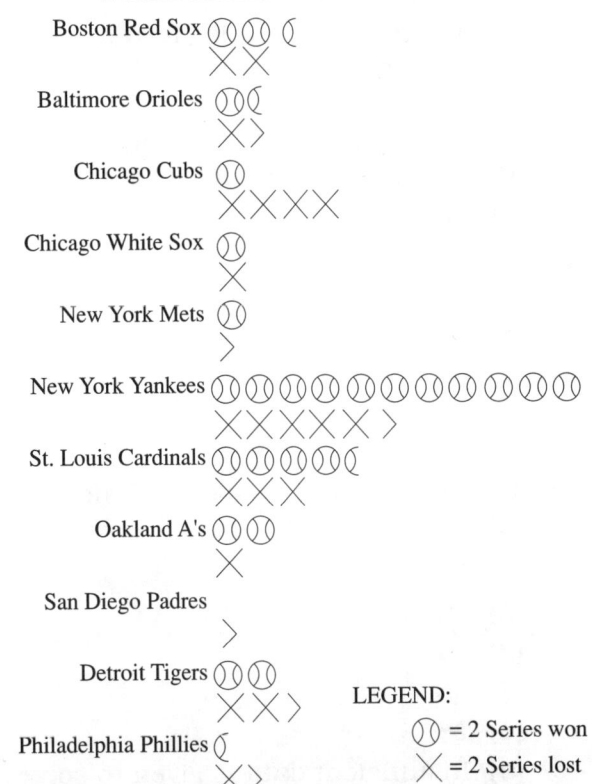

LEGEND:
🅞🅞 = 2 Series won
✕✕ = 2 Series lost

31. Which team has never won a World Series it played in?

(1) Boston Red Sox
(2) Baltimore Orioles
(3) New York Mets
(4) San Diego Padres
(5) St. Louis Cardinals

32. Which of the following expressions would show how many World Series the New York Yankees have played in?

(1) $11 + 5\frac{1}{2}$

(2) $\dfrac{11 + 5\frac{1}{2}}{2}$

(3) $11 + 5\frac{1}{2} \times 2$

(4) $2\left(11 + 5\frac{1}{2}\right)$

(5) $2\left(11 - 5\frac{1}{2}\right)$

Chapter 5: Graphs

33. What percent of its World Series have the Chicago Cubs won?

    (1) 20%
    (2) 25%
    (3) 75%
    (4) 80%
    (5) Insufficient data is given to solve the problem.

34. How many more World Series than the Orioles have the Red Sox played in?

    (1) 1
    (2) 2
    (3) 3
    (4) 6
    (5) 9

35. How many games have the Chicago White Sox played during the World Series?

    (1) 2
    (2) 4
    (3) 16
    (4) 28
    (5) Insufficient data is given to solve the problem.

36. If the Philadelphia Phillies win World Series at the same ratio as they have, how many World Series will they have to play in to win a total of six World Series?

    (1) 6
    (2) 18
    (3) 24
    (4) 36
    (5) 42

Items 37 to 40 are based on the circle graph shown below.

FACTORS IN DRIVING ACCIDENTS IN RURAL AREAS

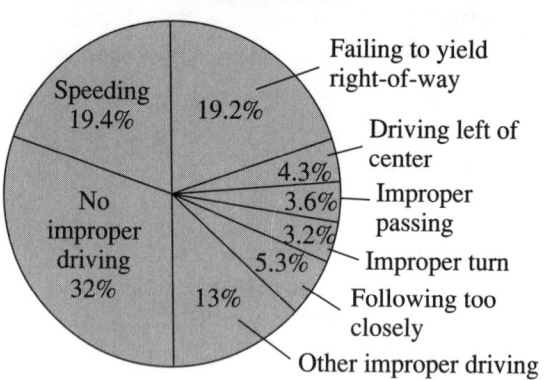

- Speeding 19.4%
- Failing to yield right-of-way 19.2%
- Driving left of center 4.3%
- Improper passing 3.6%
- Improper turn 3.2%
- Following too closely 5.3%
- Other improper driving 13%
- No improper driving 32%

37. Which fraction of the accidents were due to some form of improper driving?

    (1) $\frac{1}{5}$
    (2) $\frac{1}{4}$
    (3) $\frac{8}{25}$
    (4) $\frac{17}{25}$
    (5) $\frac{3}{4}$

38. Which of the following factors accounted for almost $\frac{1}{5}$ of the accidents?

    (1) Speeding
    (2) Driving left of center
    (3) Improper passing
    (4) Following too closely
    (5) Other improper driving

39. If 4.2 million accidents involved no improper driving, how many accidents involved some form of improper driving?

    (1) 1.344 million
    (2) 2.856 million
    (3) 8.925 million
    (4) 13.125 million
    (5) Insufficient data is given to solve the problem.

Chapter 5: Graphs

40. If $\frac{1}{5}$ of the accidents involving other improper driving were due to the driver falling asleep, which of the following expresses the percent of the total accidents due to that cause?

(1) $\frac{1}{5} \times \frac{100}{1}$
(2) $\frac{1}{5} \times \frac{13}{1}$
(3) $\frac{1}{5} \times \frac{13}{100}$
(4) $13 + \frac{1}{5} \times \frac{13}{1}$
(5) $13 - \frac{1}{5} \times \frac{13}{1}$

Items 41 to 43 are based on the circle graph shown below.

PERSONS LIVING ALONE (by age)

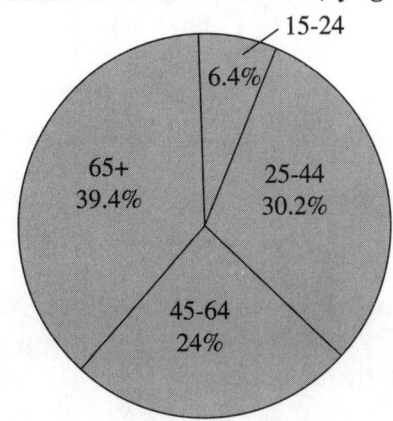

15-24: 6.4%
65+: 39.4%
25-44: 30.2%
45-64: 24%

41. What percent of the people living alone are under age 65?

(1) 4.6
(2) 6.4
(3) 36.6
(4) 54.2
(5) 60.6

42. The people living alone between the ages of 15 and 24 are approximately what fraction of the people living alone between the ages of 45 and 64?

(1) $\frac{1}{3}$
(2) $\frac{1}{4}$
(3) $\frac{1}{5}$
(4) $\frac{1}{6}$
(5) $\frac{3}{4}$

43. How many more million people living alone are between the ages of 25 and 44 than between the ages of 15 and 24?

(1) 4.998
(2) 6.432
(3) 23.8
(4) 36.6
(5) Insufficient data is given to solve the problem.

Items 44 to 48 are based on the bar graph shown below.

AVERAGE WEEKLY ALLOWANCES

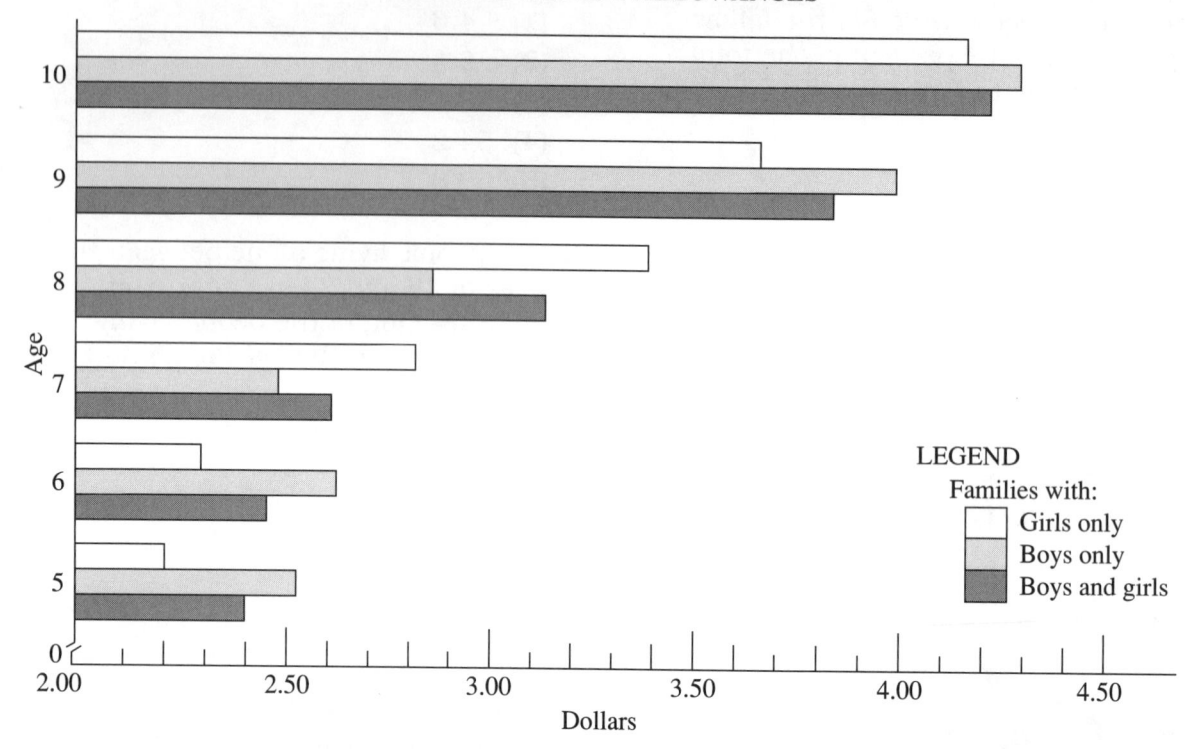

LEGEND
Families with:
- Girls only
- Boys only
- Boys and girls

44. Which of the following persons gets the largest weekly allowance?

(1) A 5-year-old in a family with boys only
(2) A 6-year-old in a family with boys only
(3) A 6-year-old in a family with boys and girls
(4) A 7-year-old in a family with girls only
(5) A 7-year-old in a family with boys and girls

45. If a family has two children, both boys, ages 7 and 10, how much more allowance than the younger boy would the older boy get?

(1) $0.85
(2) $1.18
(3) $1.60
(4) $1.73
(5) $1.80

46. Approximately what percent of the allowance of a 5-year-old girl is the allowance of a 10-year-old girl in a family without brothers?

(1) 10%
(2) $33\frac{1}{3}\%$
(3) 50%
(4) 60%
(5) Insufficient data is given to solve the problem.

47. Which of the following average allowances is less than the allowance for the person from the same type of family one year younger?

(1) A 6-year-old in a family with girls only
(2) A 7-year-old in a family with boys only
(3) A 7-year-old in a family with boys and girls
(4) A 9-year-old in a family with boys and girls
(5) A 10-year-old in a family with boys and girls

42   Chapter 5: Graphs

48. The Harmons have a 5-year-old daughter, an 8-year-old son, and a 10-year-old daughter. If they follow the average, which expression would show how much allowance they would give their children in a year?

(1) $\dfrac{\$2.20+\$2.90+\$4.20}{3}$

(2) $\dfrac{\$2.40+\$3.10+\$4.20}{52}$

(3) $52(\$2.20+\$2.90+\$4.20)$

(4) $52(\$2.40+\$3.10+\$4.20)$

(5) $\dfrac{52(\$2.40+\$3.10+\$4.20)}{3}$

Items 49 to 52 are based on the divided bar graph shown below.

GOVERNMENT EMPLOYEES

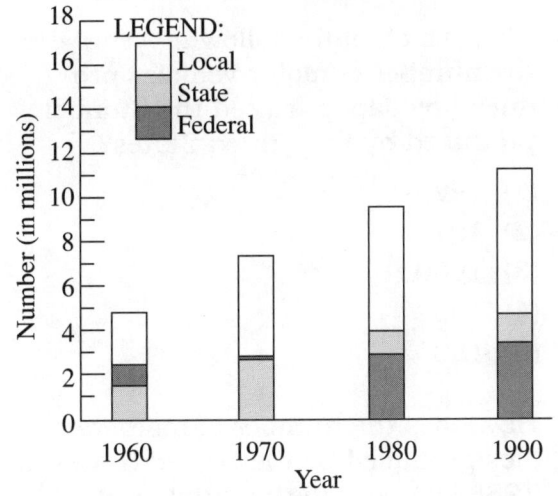

LEGEND:
Local
State
Federal

Number (in millions) vs. Year (1960, 1970, 1980, 1990)

49. Approximately how many million people were employed in state government in 1980?

(1) 1.0
(2) 3.0
(3) 3.5
(4) 10.0
(5) 16.5

50. Approximately what percent of government employees in 1960 worked for the federal government?

(1) 16%
(2) 20%
(3) 38%
(4) 55%
(5) Insufficient data is given to solve the problem.

51. The number of government employees in 1960 is approximately which fraction of the number of government employees in 1990?

(1) $\dfrac{5}{11}$
(2) $\dfrac{2}{3}$
(3) $\dfrac{3}{4}$
(4) $\dfrac{7}{8}$
(5) $\dfrac{8}{9}$

52. Which statement is true about the number of government employees?

(1) The number of employees in local government increased at a greater rate than the number in other levels of government.

(2) The number of employees in local government increased at a slower rate than the number in other levels of government.

(3) The number of employees in state government increased at a greater rate than the number in other levels of government.

(4) The number of employees in the federal government has remained the same.

(5) The number of employees in the federal government increased at a greater rate than the number in other levels of government.

Chapter 5: Graphs 43

Items 53 to 56 are based on the line graph shown below.

IMMIGRANTS ADMITTED TO THE UNITED STATES

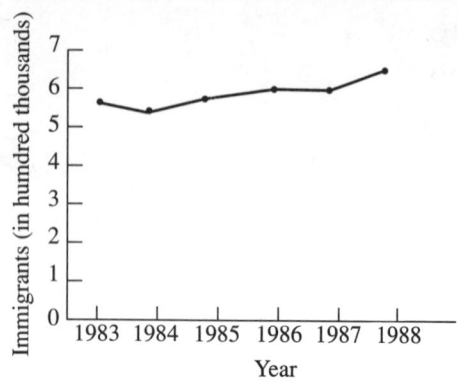

53. In which of the following years did the number of immigrants decrease from the preceding year?

(1) 1984
(2) 1985
(3) 1986
(4) 1987
(5) 1988

54. During which two years were approximately the same number of immigrants admitted to the United States?

(1) 1983 and 1984
(2) 1984 and 1985
(3) 1985 and 1986
(4) 1986 and 1987
(5) 1987 and 1988

55. How many immigrants were admitted to the United States in 1985 and 1986?

(1) Less than 120,000
(2) Less than 1,200,000
(3) More than 1,200,000
(4) Less than in 1983 and in 1984
(5) More than in 1987 and in 1988

56. Which of the following expressions would show by what percent the number of immigrants admitted to the United States in 1988 changed from the number admitted in 1983?

(1) $\dfrac{5.5}{6.5-5.5}$

(2) $\dfrac{6.5-5.5}{5.5}$

(3) $\dfrac{6.5-5.5}{6.5}$

(4) $\dfrac{100(6.5-5.5)}{5.5}$

(5) $\dfrac{100(6.5-5.5)}{6.5}$

Items 57 to 60 are based on the line graph shown below.

MOTOR VEHICLE PRODUCTION

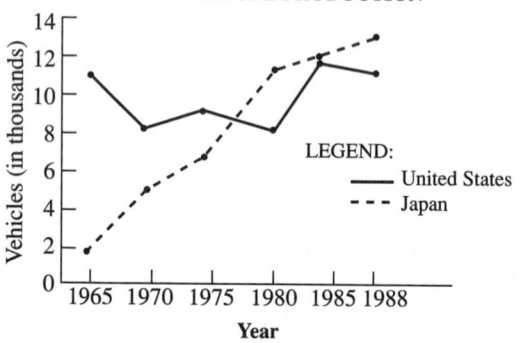

57. After which of the following years did the number of motor vehicles produced by Japan exceed the number produced by the United States?

(1) 1975
(2) 1977
(3) 1980
(4) 1982
(5) 1985

58. How does the number of motor vehicles produced by the United States in 1988 compare to the number of motor vehicles produced by Japan in the same year?

(1) 2 thousand less
(2) 2 thousand more
(3) 11 thousand less
(4) 11 thousand more
(5) 24 thousand more

44   Chapter 5: Graphs

59. What percent of the motor vehicles produced throughout the world in 1980 were produced by the United States?

(1) $1\frac{3}{8}\%$

(2) $42\frac{2}{19}\%$

(3) $37\frac{1}{2}\%$

(4) $72\frac{7}{11}\%$

(5) Insufficient data is given to solve the problem.

60. Of motor vehicles produced by the United States and Japan in 1970, which expression would show the fraction produced by Japan?

(1) $\dfrac{5}{8}$

(2) $\dfrac{5}{8+5}$

(3) $\dfrac{5}{8-5}$

(4) $\dfrac{8}{8+5}$

(5) $\dfrac{8-5}{5}$

Check your answers starting on page 117.

Chapter 5: Graphs

Chapter 6

Algebra

Level 1 — Algebra Skills

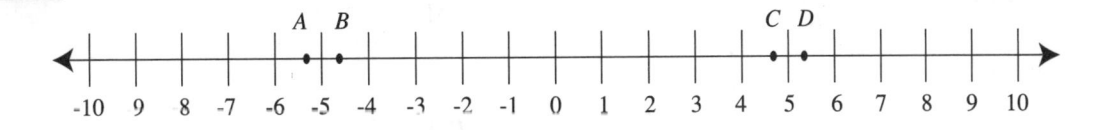

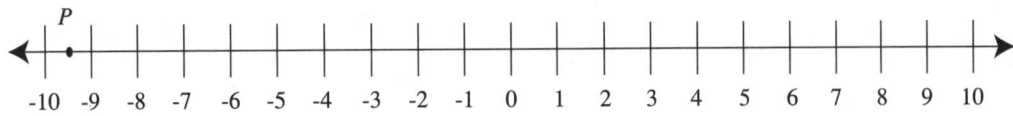

Items 1 and 2 are based on the number lines above.

1. Which point corresponds to the value $-5\frac{1}{3}$?

2. What is the value of point P?

Solve the following problems.

3. $-5 + (+4) + (-8) =$

4. $(-8) + (+15) + (-16) + (+9) =$

5. $(+9) - (-6) =$

6. $(+2) - (-1) + (-10) =$

7. $(6)(-3)\left(-\dfrac{1}{2}\right) =$

8. $(-8)(2)(-5)(-4) =$

9. $\dfrac{-28}{-7} =$

10. $\dfrac{240}{-60} =$

11. $5t + 9t =$

12. $d + (-8d) + 34d =$

13. $(5ry) - (-12ry) =$

14. $(7gk) + (-25gk) - (4gk) =$

15. $q \cdot q^3 =$

16. $(-5d^4f^2)(4d^9f^4) =$

17. $\dfrac{-18c^4d^2}{6c^6d^2} =$

18. Find the value of $y - w$ if $y = -12$ and $w = -20$.

19. Find the value of $q(q + h)$ if $q = 9$ and $h = -5$.

20. Find the value of $(b - a)^2$ if $b = -5$ and $a = -8$.

Check your answers starting on page 120.

Level 2: Algebra Application

Solve and check each equation.

1. $9x = 99$

2. $165 = w - 87$

3. $4x - 7 = 33$

4. $-2 = \dfrac{n}{3} + 1$

5. $a - 5a = 24$

6. $k - 28 = 4 - 3k$

7. $8z - 15 = 5(6 + z)$

8. $x - 9 > 47$

9. $7c + 92 \leq 141$

10. Multiply $(y + 4)(y + 6)$.

11. Multiply $(x - 3)(x + 2)$.

12. Factor $20x + 16$.

13. Factor $x^2 - 7x - 18$.

14. Solve $t^2 + 3t - 28 = 0$.

15. Solve $s^2 - 36 = 0$.

16. Simplify $\sqrt{48}$.

17. If $\frac{5}{6}h = 35$, what is the value of h?
    - (1) 7
    - (2) 29
    - (3) 42
    - (4) 175
    - (5) 210

18. If $3 - 5m = 28$, what is the value of m?
    - (1) -5
    - (2) 5
    - (3) 25
    - (4) -125
    - (5) 125

19. If $81 = \frac{2}{3}k + 9$ what is the value of k?
    - (1) 36
    - (2) 48
    - (3) 96
    - (4) 108
    - (5) 144

20. If $5x + 3 = 11x - 27$, what is the value of x?
    - (1) -2
    - (2) 2
    - (3) -5
    - (4) 5
    - (5) 30

21. If $3(r - 3) = 27$, what is the value of r?
    - (1) 6
    - (2) 9
    - (3) 12
    - (4) 54
    - (5) 108

22. If $d + 6 = 5(d - 2)$, what is the value of d?
    - (1) -1
    - (2) 2
    - (3) 4

(4) 32
(5) 48

23. Which of the following values is part of the solution set to $7y + 1 \leq 6y - 5$?

   (1) -6
   (2) -5
   (3) 0
   (4) 4
   (5) 6

24. Which of the following values is a solution to $5(q - 3) < 10$?

   (1) 3
   (2) 5
   (3) 8
   (4) 120
   (5) 126

25. Multiply $(p - 3)(p - 3)$.

   (1) $p^2 + 9$
   (2) $p^2 - 9$
   (3) $p^2 + 6p + 9$
   (4) $p^2 - 6p + 9$
   (5) $p^2 - 6p - 9$

26. Factor $m^2 - 2m$.

   (1) $2(m - m)$
   (2) $2(m^2 - m)$
   (3) $m(m - 2)$
   (4) $m(m - m)$
   (5) $2m(m - 1)$

27. Factor $h^2 - 8h - 48$.

   (1) $(h - 6)(h + 8)$
   (2) $(h + 6)(h - 8)$
   (3) $(h + 4)(h - 12)$
   (4) $(h + 3)(h - 16)$
   (5) $(h - 3)(h + 16)$

28. Which of the following values are the solutions to the equation $w^2 + 25w + 100 = 0$?

   (1) -4 only
   (2) -5 only
   (3) -5 or 20
   (4) -5 or -20
   (5) -4 or -25

29. Which of the following values are the solutions to the equation $b^2 - 2b - 15 = 0$?

   (1) -3 only
   (2) -3 or -5
   (3) -3 or 5
   (4) -5 only
   (5) -5 or 3

30. Simplify $\sqrt{162}$.

   (1) $2\sqrt{9}$
   (2) $3\sqrt{18}$
   (3) $4\sqrt{2}$
   (4) $9\sqrt{2}$
   (5) $81\sqrt{2}$

Check your answers starting on page 120.

Chapter 6, Level 2

Level 3: Algebra Problem Solving

For items 1 to 3, write an algebraic expression for each verbal expression. Use *x* to stand for the unknown.

1. Twenty-eight increased by a number

2. Nine times the quantity of a number decreased by 7

3. Twenty-one more than five-eighths of a number

For items 4 to 6, write an algebraic expression for each situation.

4. If *h* represents Don's hourly wage, what are his earnings when he works a 40-hour week?

5. Jane's age is *t* years old. What will her age be in 8 years?

6. If Joe drove 350 miles in *x* hours, what was his average speed?

For items 7 to 10, write and solve an equation for each statement.

7. Three decreased by two times a number equals 15.

8. One-half of a number plus 7 equals 22.

9. A number increased by 5 equals two times the same number decreased by 3.

10. Five times the quantity of a number increased by 5 equals 40.

For items 11 to 15, use a formula from page 139 to find a solution.

11. Bill bought three golf balls for $5.61. Find the cost of one golf ball.

12. A rectangular box has a length of 5 inches, a height of 10 inches, and a volume of 200 cubic inches. Find the width of the box in inches.

13. Tanya's savings account earned $6.84 in interest over 3 years at 6% interest. What was the principal in the account?

14. If Penelope wants to drive to a friend's house, which is 162 miles away, in 3 hours, how many miles per hour on the average should she drive?

15. A square mosaic tile has an area of 169 square centimeters. Find the measure in centimeters of a side.

16. One number is three times another number. When the larger number is decreased by 11, the result is the same as when the smaller number is decreased by 1. Find the two numbers.

17. A state budgeted two times more for highways than for education. Together, the two expenditures totaled $12 million. How much was budgeted for education?

18. To make a child's jacket Verna needed 3 yards less material than is needed for an adult's jacket. If 11 yards of material are needed to make both jackets, how much material is needed for the child's jacket?

19. The number of people who work at Joey's office is 10 more than twice the number of people who work at Heather's office. If 73 people in all work at both offices, how many work at Joey's?

20. Mark is four times as old as his son, Aaron. In 5 years, Mark's age will be 1 less than three times Aaron's age. Find both their ages.

For items 21 to 23, choose the algebraic expression that corresponds to each verbal expression.

21. The product of twelve and a number
    (1) $\dfrac{x}{12}$
    (2) $12 + x$
    (3) $12 - x$
    (4) $12x$
    (5) $\dfrac{12}{x}$

22. A number decreased by 3 all multiplied by one-half the same number
    (1) $\frac{1}{2}x \times 3$
    (2) $\frac{1}{2}x(x+3)$
    (3) $\frac{1}{2}x(x-3)$
    (4) $\frac{1}{2}x^2 - 3$
    (5) $x - \frac{1}{2}x \times 3$

23. The quantity of a number decreased by 4 divided by 6
    (1) $x - 4 - 6$
    (2) $x - \dfrac{4}{6}$
    (3) $\dfrac{x}{6} - 4$
    (4) $\dfrac{x-4}{6}$
    (5) $6(x-4)$

For items 24 to 26, choose the algebraic expression that represents each situation.

24. Marco is m years old. If his son is one-fourth his age, what is his son's age?
    (1) $\dfrac{\frac{1}{4}}{m}$
    (2) $\frac{1}{4}m$
    (3) $\frac{1}{4}+m$
    (4) $\dfrac{m}{\frac{1}{4}}$
    (5) $m - \frac{1}{4}$

25. A company employed e people. After the company lays off five people, how many people will it employ?
    (1) $5e$
    (2) $5 - e$
    (3) $e + 5$
    (4) $e - 5$
    (5) $\dfrac{e}{5}$

26. Julia bought p pounds of chicken for $4.12. What was the cost of one pound of chicken?
    (1) $p + \$4.12$
    (2) $\dfrac{p}{\$4.12}$
    (3) $\dfrac{\$4.12}{p}$
    (4) $\$4.12p$
    (5) $\$4.12 - p$

27. The quotient of a number divided by three decreased by two equals ten. Which of the following equations should be solved to find this number?
    (1) $\dfrac{3}{x} - 2 = 10$
    (2) $\dfrac{3}{x-2} = 10$
    (3) $\dfrac{\frac{3}{x}}{2} = 10$

Chapter 6, Level 3   51

(4) $\frac{x}{3} - 2 = 10$

(5) $\frac{x}{3-2} = 10$

For items 28 to 30, write and solve an equation. Then choose the answer that corresponds to the solution.

28. Thirty-two decreased by three times a number equals five.

(1) 6
(2) 9
(3) 24
(4) 27
(5) 81

29. The quantity of a number increased by fifteen divided by eight equals four.

(1) 8
(2) 17
(3) 32
(4) 60
(5) 92

30. Nine more than one-fourth of a number equals thirtynine less than the same number.

(1) 10
(2) 16
(3) 30
(4) 48
(5) 64

For items 31 to 35, use a formula from page 139 to find a solution.

31. Bob borrowed $300 for one year and paid $27 in interest. At what rate did he borrow?

(1) 2.7%
(2) 6%
(3) 9%
(4) 12%
(5) Insufficient data is given to solve the problem.

32. A dozen eggs costs $1.56. What is the cost of one egg?

(1) $0.11
(2) $0.12
(3) $0.13
(4) $0.14
(5) $0.15

33. A plane flew 3416 miles at 488 miles per hour. How many hours did the flight take?

(1) 5
(2) 5.5
(3) 6
(4) 7
(5) 8

34. Kristina borrowed $3000 for a used car. She paid a total of $840 in interest. For how many years did she borrow the money?

(1) 2
(2) 4
(3) 6
(4) 8
(5) Insufficient data is given to solve the problem.

35. The area of a triangular sail measures 150 square feet. It has a height of 25 feet. How many feet long is its base?

(1) 10
(2) 12
(3) 15
(4) 24
(5) 25

36. One number is five times another number. The smaller number increased by 41 is the same as nine times the larger number. Which of the following equations would you need to solve to find the numbers?

(1) $x = 9 \times 5x$
(2) $x = 41 + 9 \times 5x$

52   Chapter 6: Algebra

(3) $x + 41 = 9x$
   (4) $x + 41 = 9 \times 5x$
   (5) $5x + 41 = 9x$

37. The weight of the fish Lois caught was 5 pounds less than the weight of the fish Ernest caught. If their total weight was 33 pounds, how many pounds did Lois's fish weigh?

   (1) 14
   (2) 19
   (3) 28
   (4) 35
   (5) Insufficient data is given to solve the problem.

38. A service club sold popcorn to raise money for its projects. Bill sold five times as many bags of popcorn as Norm. Norm sold four bags more than Chris. Together they sold 115 bags. How many bags did Norm sell?

   (1) 13
   (2) 17
   (3) 65
   (4) 69
   (5) 91

39. Wilbur bought a new car that cost $10,250.24, including 4% sales tax. Which of the following equations would you need to solve to find how much sales tax he paid?

   (1) $0.04x = \$10,250.24$
   (2) $4x = \$10,250.24$
   (3) $x + 0.04x = \$10,250.24$
   (4) $x - 0.04x = \$10,250.24$
   (5) $x + 4x = \$10,250.24$

40. The Ferbers sold their house for $10,000 less than they paid for their new house. Their new house cost $3700 more than two times what they paid for their old house. How much did they pay for their old house?

   (1) $ 3700
   (2) $13,700
   (3) $27,400
   (4) $37,000
   (5) Insufficient data is given to solve the problem.

Check your answers starting on page 122.

Chapter 7

Geometry

Level 1 — Geometry Skills

1. What type of angle is angle *ABC*?

2. An angle measures 180°. What type of angle is it?

3. If angle *GHJ* measures 180°, what does angle *KHJ* measure?

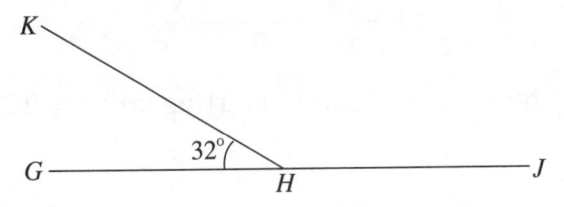

Items 4 and 5 are based on the following figure.

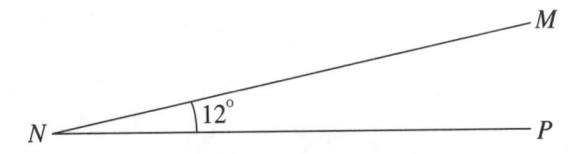

4. What type of angle is angle *MNP*?

5. What would an angle complementary to angle *MNP* measure?

Items 6 and 7 are based on the following figure.

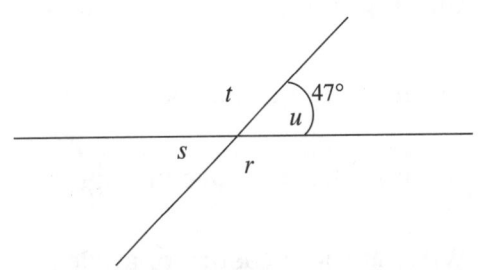

6. What is the measure of angle *s*?
7. Which angle is vertical to angle *t*?
8. What type of angle is angle *XYZ*?

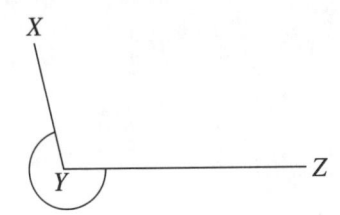

Items 9 to 12 are based on the following figure.

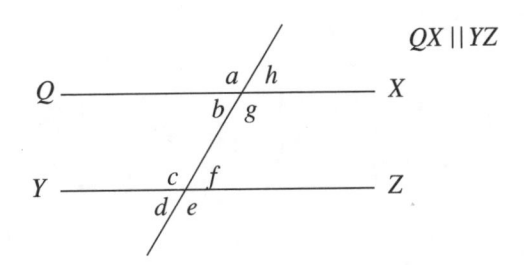

QX || YZ

9. Which angle corresponds to angle *d*?

10. What is the relationship of angles *c* and *g*?

Chapter 7, Level 1   55

11. Which angle is an alternate exterior angle of angle *h*?

12. What is the relationship of angles *c* and *f*?

Items 13 to 16 are based on the following figure.

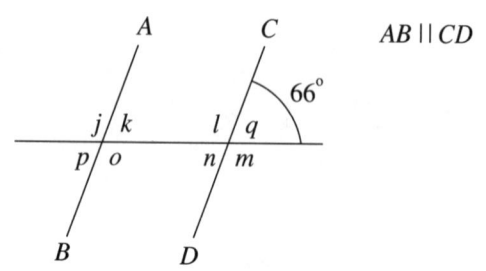

13. What is the measure of angle *n*?

14. What is the measure of angle *m*?

15. What is the measure of angle *k*?

16. What is the measure of angle *p*?

17. What is the measure of angle *A*?

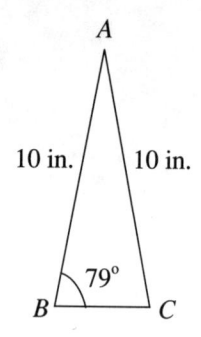

18. In a right triangle, if one of the acute angles measures 27°, what is the measure of the other acute angle?

19. In triangle *TPW*, angle *T* measures 50° and angle *P* measures 97°. Which is the longest side?

20. What type of triangle is *WXY*?

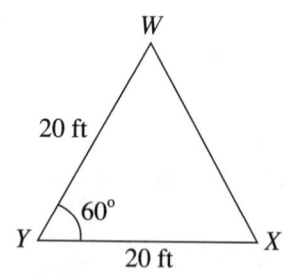

Check your answers starting on page 124.

56   Chapter 7: Geometry

Level 2: Geometry Application

1. Triangle ABC is similar to triangle DEF. What is the measure of angle D?

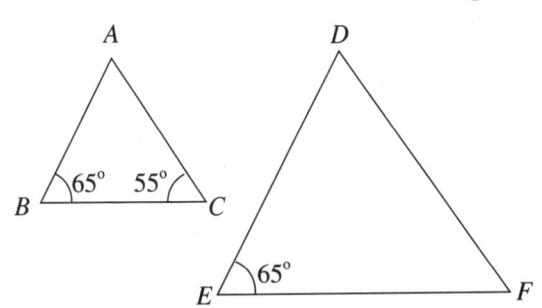

2. Triangle GIH is similar to triangle LNM. What is the length in inches of LN?

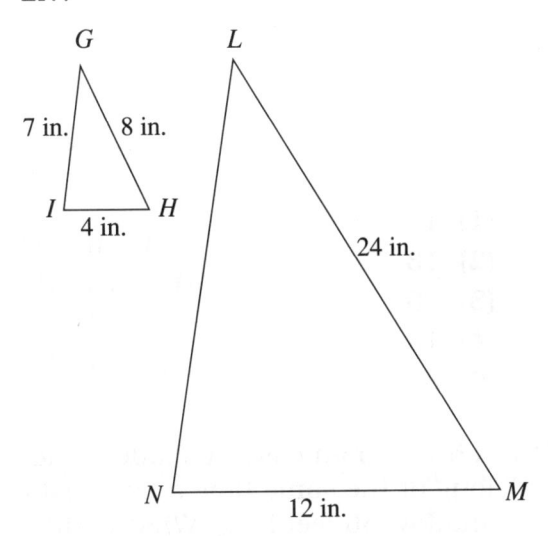

For items 3 to 5, determine whether the pairs of triangles are congruent. If they are, tell which requirement (SAS, ASA, or SSS) is satisfied. If they are not, state which requirement is not satisfied.

3.

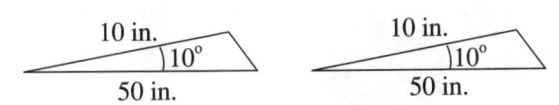

4.

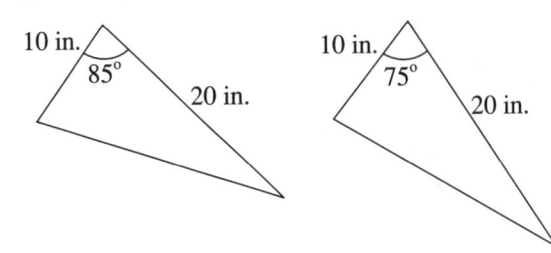

5.

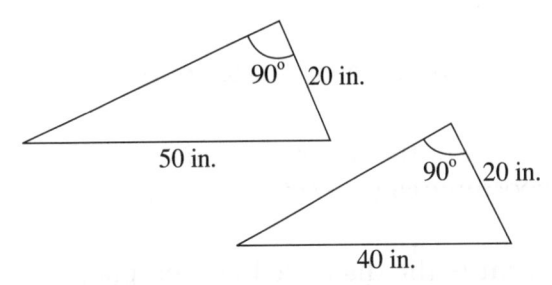

6. What is the length in inches of the hypotenuse of the triangle below?

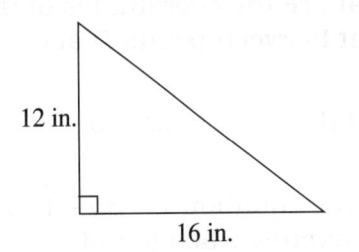

7. What is the length in inches of AC?

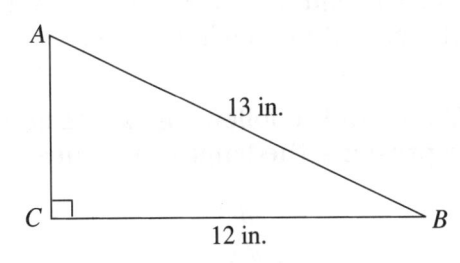

8. The hypotenuse of a right triangle measures 17 inches, and one leg measures 15 inches. Find the length of the other leg.

24. What are the coordinates of point *I*?

   (1) (10, 4)
   (2) (4, 10)
   (3) (-4, 10)
   (4) (10, -4)
   (5) (-10, 4)

25. Which of the following expressions would be used to find the distance between points *A* and *B*?

   (1) $d = \sqrt{[7-(-4)]^2 + [10-(-8)]^2}$

   (2) $d = \sqrt{[-4-(-8)]^2 + (7-10)^2}$

   (3) $d = \sqrt{[7-(-8)]^2 + (-4-10)^2}$

   (4) $d = \sqrt{(-4-8)^2 + (7-10)^2}$

   (5) $d = \sqrt{[-4+(-8)]^2 + (7+10)^2}$

26. What are the coordinates of the midpoint between points *C* and *K*?

   (1) (1, 4)
   (2) (-2, -4)
   (3) (-6, -2)
   (4) (-6, -4)
   (5) (-12, -4)

27. What is the slope of *DG*?

   (1) $\frac{1}{5}$
   (2) $-\frac{1}{5}$
   (3) $-\frac{1}{10}$
   (4) 5
   (5) -5

28. What are the coordinates of the *y*-intercept for the equation $x = 4y + 12$?

   (1) (0, -3)
   (2) (0, 12)
   (3) (-3, 0)
   (4) (12, 0)
   (5) (12, -3)

29. For the equation $y = \frac{x}{3} + 6$, find the value of *x* when $y = 12$.

   (1) 10
   (2) 18
   (3) 30
   (4) 36
   (5) 48

30. Which of the following points is on the graph of the equation $y = x^2 - 5x + 6$?

   (1) (0, -2)
   (2) (-1, 2)
   (3) (1, -2)
   (4) (2, 0)
   (5) (-2, -1)

Check your answers starting on page 124.

Level 3: Geometry Problem Solving

1. The triangle below has an area of 77 square inches. What is its height in inches?

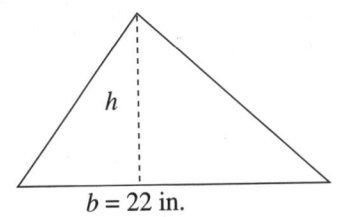

   (triangle with h, b = 22 in.)

2. An equilateral triangle has a perimeter of 216 inches. What does each side measure in inches?

3. The circumference of a fountain is 31.4 feet. What is the fountain's diameter?

4. The perimeter of Liz's living room is 88 feet. If the room is a rectangle with a length of 24 feet, what is its width?

5. Find the measure of one side of a square that has a perimeter of 64 inches.

6. The square and the rectangle below have the same area. Find the width in feet of the rectangle.

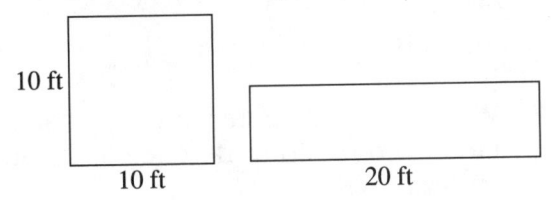

   (square 10 ft × 10 ft; rectangle 20 ft long)

7. The volume of the packing crate below is 30 cubic feet. What is its height?

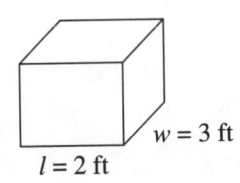

   ($l = 2$ ft, $w = 3$ ft)

8. An isosceles triangle has a perimeter of 28 inches. If two sides have a length of 12 inches, what is the length of the third side?

9. The perimeter of Sam's living room is 40 feet. The length is 4 feet longer than the width. What are the dimensions in feet of the living room?

10. The perimeter of a triangle is 105 inches. One side is 5 inches longer than the shortest side. The longest side is twice as long as the shortest side. How many inches long are the sides?

11. A rectangle with an area of 128 square inches has a length twice the measure of its width. How many inches wide is it?

12. The rectangular container shown below has a volume of 200 cubic inches. How many inches high is it?

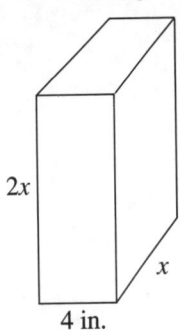

    ($2x$, x, 4 in.)

13. A triangle has an area of 224 square inches. The ratio of its base to its height is 7:4. Find the measurement in inches of its base and height.

14. A room is three times as long as it is wide. If its area is 108 square feet, find its measurements in feet.

Chapter 7, Level 3   61

15. A walk around the block Bruce lives on covers a distance of 1200 feet. The width of the block is 50 feet shorter than the length. Find the width of the block in feet.

16. If the figure shown below has an area of 2646 cubic inches, what is its length and height in inches?

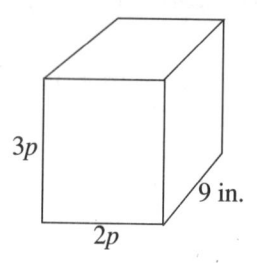

(figure: box with dimensions $3p$, $2p$, and 9 in.)

17. Express in simplest form the length of the hypotenuse of the triangle shown below.

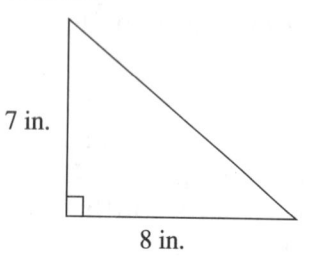

(right triangle with legs 7 in. and 8 in.)

18. Find the length of the diagonal of the square shown below. Express the answer in simplest form.

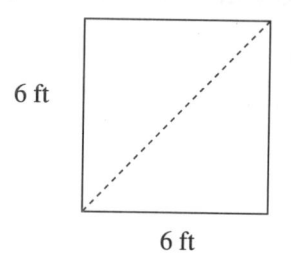

(square 6 ft by 6 ft with diagonal)

19. What is the distance in miles from Plainville to Roctown via Highway 7D? Express the answer in simplest form.

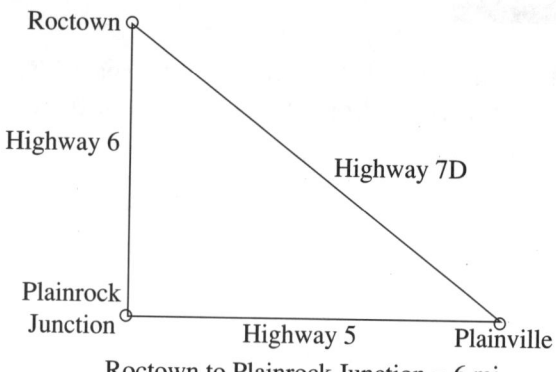

(triangle diagram: Roctown, Plainrock Junction, Plainville connected by Highway 6, Highway 5, Highway 7D)

Roctown to Plainrock Junction = 6 mi
Plainville to Plainrock Junction = 10 mi

20. The diagram shown below is of a planned football play. How many yards could be gained by this play? Express the answer in simplest form.

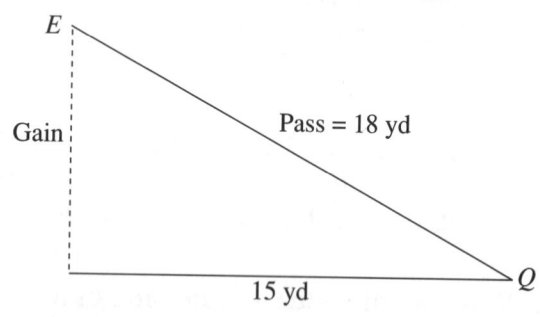

(right triangle: Gain (E), Pass = 18 yd, 15 yd, Q)

21. A square has a perimeter of 14.92 feet. How many feet long is a side?

 (1) 3.73
 (2) 4.07
 (3) 5.46
 (4) 6.03
 (5) 8.46

22. What is the diameter in meters of a circle with a circumference of 12.56 meters?

 (1) 2
 (2) 3
 (3) 4
 (4) 39
 (5) Insufficient data is given to solve the problem.

23. A rectangular garden has an area of 96 square feet. If it is 6 feet wide, which of the following expressions would show its length in feet?

(1) $\dfrac{96}{6}$

(2) $\dfrac{96}{2(6)}$

(3) $\dfrac{96-6}{2}$

(4) $\sqrt{96-6}$

(5) $\dfrac{96-2(6)}{2}$

24. A triangle has an area of 36 square inches. What is its height in inches?

(1) 6
(2) 9
(3) 12
(4) 18
(5) Insufficient data is given to solve the problem.

25. Which of the following expressions would show the radius in centimeters of a circle with an area of 62.8 square centimeters?

(1) $3.14\sqrt{62.8}$

(2) $\dfrac{62.8}{2(3.14)}$

(3) $\dfrac{\sqrt{62.8}}{3.14}$

(4) $\sqrt{\dfrac{62.8}{3.14}}$

(5) $\dfrac{62.8}{3.14}$

26. The rectangle and the triangle below have the same area. Find the height in feet of the triangle.

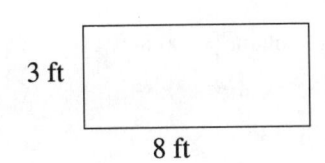

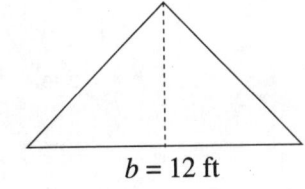

3 ft
8 ft
$b = 12$ ft

(1) 2
(2) 3
(3) 4
(4) 6
(5) Insufficient data is given to solve the problem.

27. The volume of the rectangular container shown below is 360 cubic inches. Which of the following expressions would show the container's length in inches?

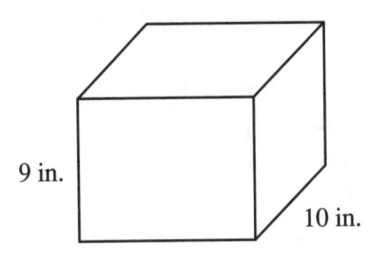

9 in.
10 in.

(1) $\dfrac{360}{9}$

(2) $\dfrac{360}{10}$

(3) $\dfrac{360}{10+9}$

(4) $\dfrac{360}{10\times 9}$

(5) $\dfrac{9\times 360}{10}$

28. An isosceles triangle has a perimeter of 40 inches. Its longest side is 16 inches long. What are the lengths in inches of each of its other sides?

(1) 8
(2) 12
(3) 20
(4) 24
(5) Insufficient data is given to solve the problem.

Chapter 7, Level 3

29. A triangle has a perimeter of 79 inches. One side of the triangle is 20 inches long. A second side is 3 inches longer than the third side. How many inches long is the third side?

   (1) 28
   (2) 31
   (3) 38
   (4) 41
   (5) Insufficient data is given to solve the problem.

30. A rectangle has a perimeter of 126 inches. Its length is three inches less than five times its width. Which of the following expressions would you need to solve to find how many inches long it is?

   (1) $126 = (5x + 3) \cdot x$
   (2) $126 = (5x - 3) + x$
   (3) $126 = 2(5x + 3) + 2x$
   (4) $126 = 2(5x - 3) + 2x$
   (5) $126 = 2(x - 3) + 2(5x)$

31. What is the width in inches of the rectangle shown below?

   Area = 37.5 in.², x, $6x$

   (1) 2.5
   (2) 3.2
   (3) 4.6
   (4) 5.1
   (5) 6.0

32. Which of the following expressions would show the measure in inches of the longest side of the triangle below?

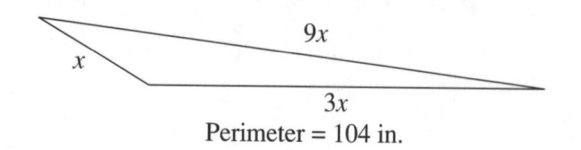

   x, $9x$, $3x$, Perimeter = 104 in.

   (1) $\dfrac{104}{9}$
   (2) $\dfrac{104}{13}$
   (3) $9 \times \dfrac{104}{4}$
   (4) $9 \times \dfrac{104}{13}$
   (5) $9 \times \dfrac{104}{12}$

33. A triangle has a base/height ratio of 4:3. If it has an area of 24 square inches, what is the length of its base in inches?

   (1) 2
   (2) 4
   (3) 6
   (4) 8
   (5) Insufficient data is given to solve the problem.

34. Carry's lot is one-half as wide as it is long. How many feet wide is the lot?

   (1) 50
   (2) 100
   (3) 150
   (4) 200
   (5) Insufficient data is given to solve the problem.

35. What is the height in cubic inches of the rectangular container shown below?

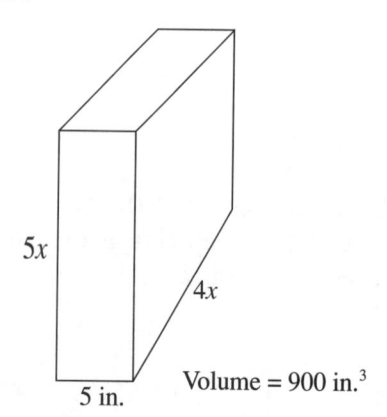

   $5x$, $4x$, 5 in., Volume = 900 in.³

64   Chapter 7: Geometry

(1) 3
(2) 9
(3) 12
(4) 15
(5) 17

36. What is the length in inches of the rectangle shown below?

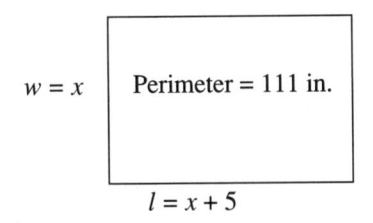

$w = x$ | Perimeter = 111 in.
$l = x + 5$

(1) 15.25
(2) 25.25
(3) 30.25
(4) 50.5
(5) 60.5

37. Express in simplest form the length of the hypotenuse of the triangle shown below.

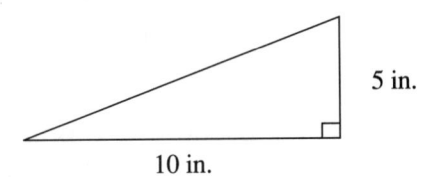

5 in.
10 in.

(1) 5
(2) 25
(3) $5\sqrt{5}$
(4) $\sqrt{125}$
(5) 125

38. Which of the following expressions represents the length of the diagonal of the rectangle shown below?

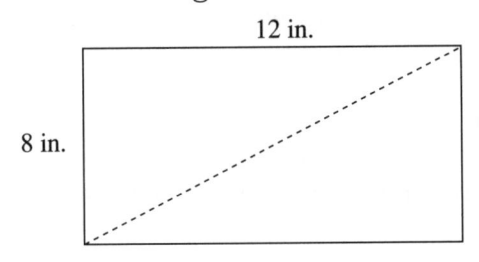

12 in.
8 in.

(1) $\sqrt{8+12}$
(2) $\dfrac{8+12}{2}$
(3) $8^2 + 12^2$
(4) $(2 \times 8) + (2 \times 12)$
(5) $\sqrt{8^2 + 12^2}$

39. How many feet above the ground is Phil's seat?

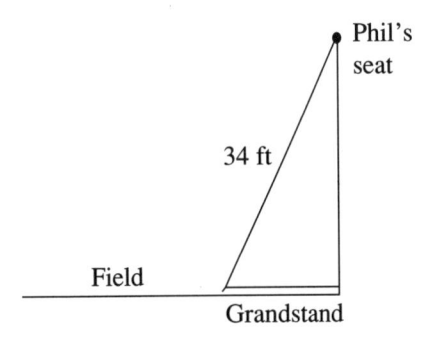

Phil's seat
34 ft
Field
Grandstand

(1) 18
(2) 24
(3) 30
(4) 34
(5) Insufficient data is given to solve the problem.

40. Martin drove 9 miles north and 13 miles west. In simplest form, what is the shortest distance from his starting point to his endpoint?

(1) $\sqrt{22}$
(2) $2\sqrt{11}$
(3) $3\sqrt{13}$
(4) $5\sqrt{10}$
(5) Insufficient data is given to solve the problem.

Check your answers starting on page 126.

(1) 80°
(2) 50°
(3) 60°
(4) 100°
(5) Insufficient data is given to solve the problem.

Item 7 is based on the following table.

MATERIAL NEEDED (in yards)

SIZE	SHIRT	SUIT	DRESS	SKIRT	PANTS
7	4	8	8	5	3
8	5	10	9.5	7	4
9	6	12	11	9	5
10	7	14	13.5	11	6

7. If Rick Carberra wants to make two size 9 suits, a size 7 skirt, a size 10 dress, and three size 8 pants, how many yards of material should he get, assuming no waste?

(1) 33
(2) 44
(3) 54.5
(4) 59
(5) 76

Item 8 is based on the following figure.

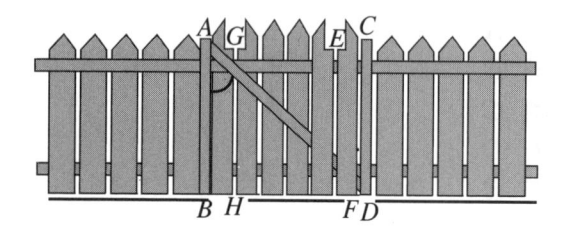

8. If post *AB* and post *CD* are perpendicular to the ground line, which of the following statements must be true?

(1) Posts *AB* and *CD* are parallel to the ground.
(2) Posts *AB* and *CD* are parallel to each other.
(3) Posts *AB* and *CD* are perpendicular to each other.
(4) Posts *AB* and *CD* are perpendicular to *GF*.
(5) *GF* is perpendicular to the ground.

Item 9 is based on the following table, which shows the sizes of four milk bottles and the amount of milk left in each of them.

Bottle	Size (in ounces)	Fraction Full
A	16	$\frac{7}{8}$
B	32	$\frac{2}{5}$
C	64	$\frac{1}{4}$
D	128	$\frac{3}{16}$

9. Which of the following sequences shows the correct order of bottles containing the most to least milk?

(1) D, C, A, B
(2) D, C, B, A
(3) D, A, B, C
(4) B, A, D, C
(5) A, B, D, C

Items 10 and 11 are based on the following graph.

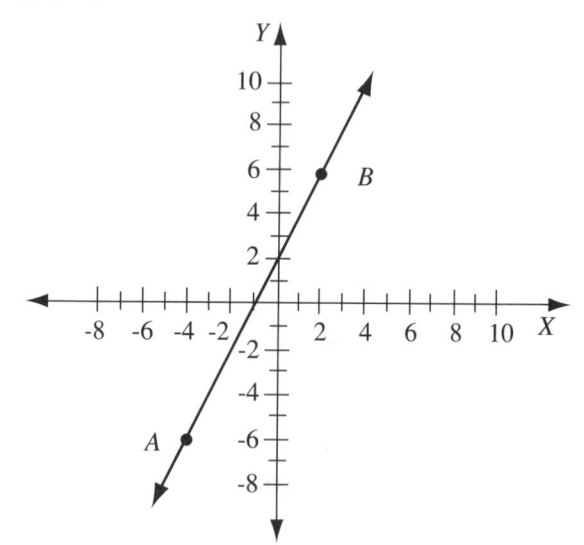

10. Which of the following expressions would show the slope of *AB*?

(1) $\frac{2-(-4)}{6-(-6)}$

(2) $\frac{2+(-4)}{6+(-6)}$

(3) $\frac{6-(-6)}{-4-2}$

68   Half-Length Practice Test

(4) $\dfrac{6+(-6)}{2+(-4)}$

(5) $\dfrac{6-(-6)}{2-(-4)}$

11. Using the formula for the midpoint of a segment,
$M = \left(\dfrac{x_1+x_2}{2}, \dfrac{y_1+y_2}{2}\right)$,
find the midpoint of segment AB.

(1) (0, 1)
(2) (0, -1)
(3) (1, -1)
(4) (1, 0)
(5) (-1, 0)

12. During one trading day a total of 1.05×10^8 issues were traded on the stock exchange. Which of the following numbers equals that amount?

(1) 10.5
(2) 84
(3) 10,500,000
(4) 105,000,000
(5) 840,000,000

13. At a football game Ed Delozier purchased a program with a number printed inside it. Five times during the game a number was announced and a prize was awarded to the person who had that number in his or her program. A total of 25,000 programs were printed from which the numbers were drawn, but only 15,000 were sold. What were Ed's chances of winning a prize?

(1) $\dfrac{3}{5}$
(2) $\dfrac{1}{3000}$
(3) $\dfrac{1}{5000}$
(4) $\dfrac{1}{25,000}$
(5) Insufficient data is given to solve the problem.

14. Walter Seelmore has the choice of two types of material with which to insulate his attic. To get the same insulation value as 3 inches of type W insulation, he would need 5 inches of type F insulation. How many inches of type F insulation would he need to get the same insulation value as 21 inches of type W?

(1) $12\tfrac{3}{5}$
(2) 35
(3) 63
(4) 105
(5) Insufficient data is given to solve the problem.

15. A flagpole that is 12 feet tall casts a 15-foot shadow. At the same time, the house behind it casts a 25-foot shadow. What is the height of the house in feet?

(1) 20
(2) 22
(3) 28
(4) 30
(5) $31\tfrac{1}{4}$

16. Starting with a full tank of 25 gallons of gasoline, Rudy Gold drove his truck 100 miles. At the end of this trip, g gallons of gasoline remained in the tank. Which of the following expressions would show the truck's miles per gallon?

(1) $\dfrac{100}{25-g}$
(2) $\dfrac{100}{25+g}$
(3) $\dfrac{100}{g-25}$
(4) $25 - 100g$
(5) $\dfrac{25-g}{100}$

Half-Length Practice Test 69

17. A book of 20 stamps cost $5.80. If s equals the price of a single stamp, which of the following equations should be used to find the price of a single stamp?

    (1) $\dfrac{20}{s} = \$5.80$

    (2) $20s = \$5.80$

    (3) $\dfrac{s}{\$5.80}$

    (4) $\$5.80s = 20$

    (5) Insufficient data is given to solve the problem.

18. Roberta Perkins currently employs 14 people in her business. That is two more than three times the number of employees she had when she started her business. Which of the following equations could you solve to find how many employees she had when she started?

    (1) $\dfrac{3}{x} - 2 = 14$
    (2) $3x - 2 = 14$
    (3) $3x + 2 = 14$
    (4) $x + 2 = 14$
    (5) $x + 3x + 2 = 14$

19. At her job Marilyn Miller spends four times as much time with customers and three times as much time doing paperwork than she does on the telephone. How many hours a week does she spend on the telephone?

    (1) 5
    (2) 8
    (3) 15
    (4) 20
    (5) Insufficient data is given to solve the problem.

20. A department store offered a special promotion during which it gave a 10% discount on all purchases over $200. It programmed its cash registers to automatically apply the discount. If p equals purchases, which of the following formulas did it use to recognize purchases that qualified for the discount?

    (1) $p > 10$
    (2) $p < 10$
    (3) $p = 200$
    (4) $p > 200$
    (5) $p < 200$

21. How many pounds do 6 cases of coffee weigh if each case holds twelve 3-pound cans?

    (1) 4
    (2) 18
    (3) 36
    (4) 72
    (5) 216

22. In a triathlon, Laura Brown swam at 3 miles per hour for 40 minutes, ran at 6 miles per hour for 3 hours 10 minutes, and rode a bicycle at 9 miles per hour for 2 hours. Which of the following expressions would show how many miles she traveled altogether?

    (1) $3 + 6 + 9$
    (2) $(3+6+9)\left(\tfrac{2}{3}+3\tfrac{1}{6}+2\right)$
    (3) $3\left(\tfrac{2}{3}+3\tfrac{1}{6}+2\right)$
    (4) $3\left(\tfrac{2}{3}\right)+6\left(3\tfrac{1}{6}\right)+9(2)$
    (5) $3(40)+6(310)+9(2)$

23. $\dfrac{56a^3b^{14}c^{84}}{8a^2b^7c^{12}}$ is equal to which of the following expressions?

    (1) $7a^{1.5}b^2c^7$
    (2) $7a^2b^2c^7$
    (3) $7ab^7c^{72}$
    (4) $48ab^7c^7$
    (5) $48a^2b^7c^{72}$

Item 24 is based on the following figure.

HELICOPTER LANDING PAD

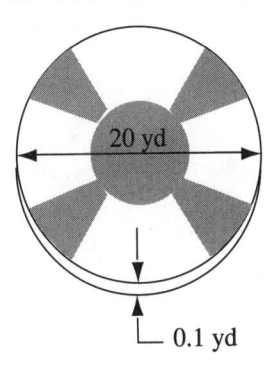

20 yd

0.1 yd

24. Assuming no waste, how many cubic yards of concrete were used in building the helicopter landing pad?

(1) 3.14
(2) 9.42
(3) 31.4
(4) 94.2
(5) Insufficient data is given to solve the problem.

Item 25 is based on the following figure.

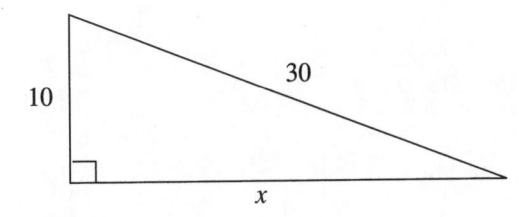

10, 30, x

25. Which of the following statements is true?

(1) $x = 30 + 10$
(2) $x^2 = 30^2 - 10^2$
(3) $x^2 = 30^2 + 10^2$
(4) $30^2 = x^2 - 10^2$
(5) $30^2 = 10^2 - x^2$

Item 26 is based on the following figure.

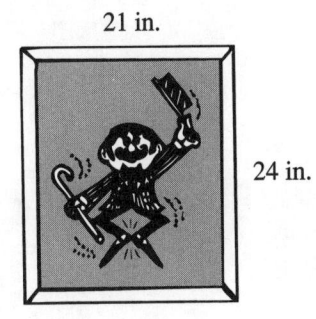

21 in.
24 in.

26. Which of the following expressions would show the least number of square inches of glass needed to cover the picture?

(1) $2 \times 21 \times 24$
(2) $2(21 + 24)$
(3) $2(21) + 2(24)$
(4) 21×24
(5) $21^2 + 24^2$

Items 27 and 28 are based on the following graph.

COMPUTER SOFTWARE PROGRAMS SOLD

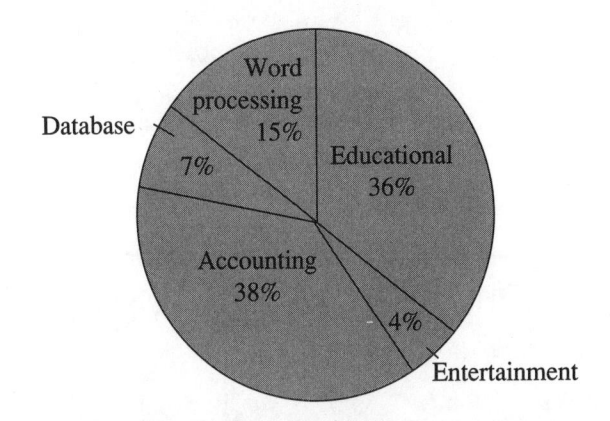

Word processing 15%
Database 7%
Educational 36%
Accounting 38%
Entertainment 4%

27. How many more word-processing than database programs were sold?

(1) 8
(2) 22
(3) 800
(4) 2200
(5) Insufficient data is given to solve the problem.

28. A computer store sold its software at exactly the percentages shown on the graph. If it sold 324 educational programs, which of the following expressions would show the number of accounting programs it sold?

(1) $36(324 \times 38)$
(2) $36\left(\dfrac{324}{38}\right)$
(3) $38(324 \times 36)$

Half-Length Practice Test   71

(4) $\dfrac{324}{38 \times 36}$

(5) $\dfrac{324 \times 38}{36}$

Check your answers starting on page 129.

Half-Length Practice Test

Performance Analysis Chart

DIRECTIONS:

Circle the number of each item that you got correct on the test. Count how many items you got correct in each row; count how many items you got correct in each column. Write the number correct per row and column as the numerator in the fraction in the appropriate "Total Correct" box. (The denominators represent the total number of items in the row or column.) Write the grand total correct over the denominator **28** at the lower right corner of the chart. (For example, if you got **24** items correct, write **24** so that the fraction reads **24/28**.) Item numbers in boldface represent items based on graphic material.

Item Type	Arithmetic (Chapters 1-5)	Algebra (Chapter 6)	Geometry (Chapter 7)	Total Correct
Skills		**5**, 23	**6, 8**	—/4
Application	3, 12, 13, 14, **24, 26**	1, 2	**10, 11**, 15, **25**	—/12
Problem Solving	4, 7, 9, 21, 22, **27, 28**	16, 17, 18, 19, 20		—/12
Total Correct	—/13	—/9	—/6	—/28

The chapters named in parentheses indicate where in the math instruction of *The Cambridge Comprehensive Program* and *The Cambridge Program for the Mathematics Test* you can find specific instruction about the various areas of mathematics.

On the chart, items are classified as Skills, Application, or Problem Solving. In the mathematics instruction chapters of both textbooks, the three problem types are covered in different levels:

      Skills items are covered in Level 1.

      Application items are covered in Level 2.

      Problem Solving items are covered in Level 3.

For example, the skills needed to solve item 10 are covered in Level 2 of Chapter 7. To locate the chapters in which arithmetic items are addressed, reread the problem to see what kind of numbers (whole numbers, fractions, etc.) are used, and then go to the designated level of the appropriate chapter.

Full-Length Practice Test

DIRECTIONS:

Choose the one best answer for each item.

Items 1 to 4 are based on the following information.

The Booster Bank offers a special certificate of deposit with the interest rate tied to the performance of its local basketball team.

The bank pays a minimum of 6% interest on the CDs, but the rate is subject to increase. If the team has a winning record, the rate is raised to 6.25%. If the team wins the division, the rate is increased an additional 0.25%. If the team wins the championship, the rate is 6.75%.

The CD accounts can be opened for 3 months, 6 months, 1 year, or 5 years only. A depositor receives a free basketball when opening an account of $1000 or more.

1. If the team does not have a winning record, how much interest would a 1-year $1450 CD earn?

    (1) $87
    (2) $90.62
    (3) $94.25
    (4) $96.06
    (5) Insufficient data is given to solve the problem.

2. Terril is opening a 3-month CD account for $800. If the team wins the championship, how much interest will he earn?

    (1) $12.50
    (2) $13.50
    (3) $18.00
    (4) $54.00
    (5) Insufficient data is given to solve the problem.

3. Wilma earned $150 interest on her 5-year CD of $480. Which of the following expressions shows the rate of interest she received?

    (1) $\dfrac{5}{\$150 \times \$480}$
    (2) $\dfrac{\$480 \times \$150}{5}$
    (3) $\$480 \times \$150 \times 5$
    (4) $\dfrac{\$150}{5 \times \$480}$
    (5) $\dfrac{\$480}{5 \times \$150}$

4. Bernice is opening a 6-month CD for $1700. How much money will she have after 6 months if the team wins the division?

    (1) $1755.25
    (2) $1756.31
    (3) $1802
    (4) $1812.63
    (5) Insufficient data is given to solve the problem.

5. Simplify $2e + 4f + 3e - 7f$.

    (1) $5e - 3f$
    (2) $5e + 11f$
    (3) $5e^2 - 3f^2$
    (4) $16ef$
    (5) $168ef$

Item 6 is based on the following figure.

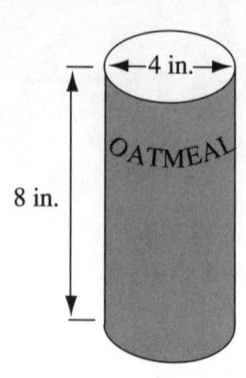

6. What is the volume in cubic inches of the oatmeal container?

   (1) 15.14
   (2) 37.68
   (3) 50.24
   (4) 100.48
   (5) 401.92

7. Alvin rode his bicycle 31.5 miles in 3.5 hours. What was his average speed in miles per hour?

   (1) 9
   (2) 28
   (3) 35
   (4) 110.25
   (5) Insufficient data is given to solve the problem.

8. A girl casts a 6-foot shadow at the same time that a flagpole casts a 36-foot shadow. What is the height in feet of the flagpole?

   (1) 6
   (2) 30
   (3) 42
   (4) 48
   (5) Insufficient data is given to solve the problem.

9. Maria entered a contest at a grocery store in which the number of cans in a barrel had to be guessed. The winner was to be chosen from all the correct entries. Maria placed an entry every time she went shopping and 2 out of her 15 entries were correct. If there were a total of 36 correct entries, including hers, what were her chances of winning?

   (1) $\frac{1}{18}$
   (2) $\frac{2}{15}$
   (3) $\frac{5}{12}$
   (4) $\frac{13}{26}$
   (5) Insufficient data is given to solve the problem.

10. Alice bought m cucumbers for $1.32. Which of the following expresses the cost of one cucumber?

    (1) $m + \$1.32$
    (2) $m - \$1.32$
    (3) $\$132m$
    (4) $\dfrac{\$1.32}{m}$
    (5) $\dfrac{m}{\$1.32}$

11. Fred bought four 3-pound bags of apples and two 10-pound bags of oranges. What is the total weight in pounds of the fruit he bought?

    (1) 13
    (2) 22
    (3) 23
    (4) 32
    (5) 78

Item 12 is based on the following figure.

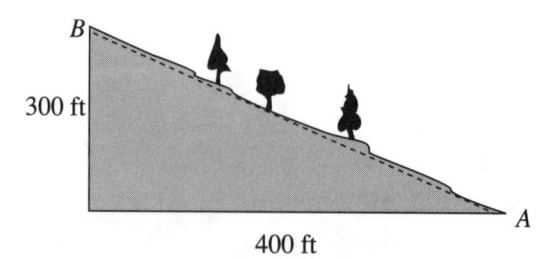

12. Albert is standing at point A. Bruce is standing on top of the hill at point B. How many feet apart are they in straight-line distance?

    (1) 10
    (2) 100
    (3) 500

76   Full-Length Practice Test

(4) 700

(5) Insufficient data is given to solve the problem.

13. Howard rides the bus for 25 minutes each day, 5 days a week. How much time does he spend on the bus each week?

   (1) 1 hour 25 minutes
   (2) 2 hours
   (3) 2 hours 5 minutes
   (4) 2 hours 50 minutes
   (5) 3 hours 25 minutes

14. A parsec is 1.92×10^{13} miles. It's used in measuring the distance between stars. If written out as a number, how many zeros would follow the digit 2?

   (1) 10
   (2) 11
   (3) 12
   (4) 13
   (5) 14

Item 15 is based on the following figure.

PICNIC TABLE

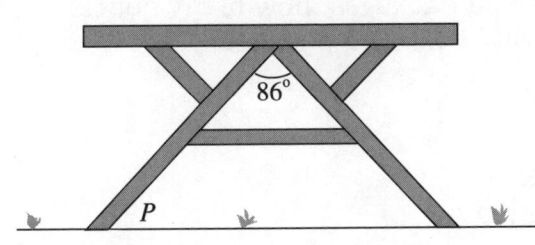

15. Which of the following degrees will angle *P* measure if the picnic table legs are of equal length?

   (1) 43
   (2) 47
   (3) 86
   (4) 94
   (5) 133

Item 16 is based on the following chart.

DRIVING TEST RESULTS

Name	Score
Mary	98
Bill	76
Harold	90
Vincent	67
Kevin	92
Wendy	88
Beth	85

16. Who received the median score on the driving test?

   (1) Beth
   (2) Bill
   (3) Kevin
   (4) Vincent
   (5) Wendy

17. What is the value of $i(i - k)$ if $i = -3$ and $k = 5$?

   (1) -6
   (2) 6
   (3) -10
   (4) -24
   (5) 24

Item 18 is based on the following figure.

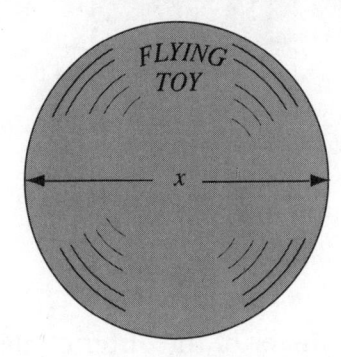

18. If the area of the flying disk toy is 113.04 square inches, what is the value of *x* in inches?

   (1) 6
   (2) 12
   (3) 10
   (4) 36
   (5) Insufficient data is given to solve the problem.

Full-Length Practice Test 77

Item 19 is based on the following chart.

Dieter	Pounds Lost/ Targeted Weight Loss
A	$\frac{7}{12}$
B	$\frac{2}{3}$
C	$\frac{11}{18}$
D	$\frac{23}{36}$
E	$\frac{5}{9}$

19. Which of the following sequences shows the correct order of dieters from most to least successful in attaining the targeted weight loss?

    (1) E, A, B, C, D
    (2) D, C, B, A, E
    (3) D, C, A, E, B
    (4) B, E, A, C, D
    (5) B, D, C, A, E

Items 20 and 21 are based on the following figure.

BASKETBALL COURT

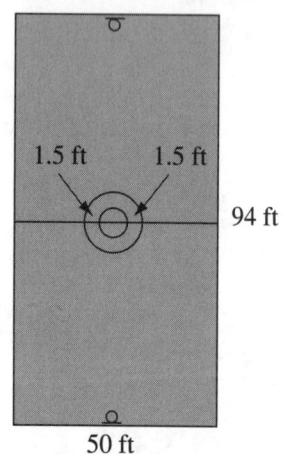

20. The diameter of the outer circle is 7 feet. How many feet long is the radius of the inner circle?

    (1) 2
    (2) 2.75
    (3) 3
    (4) 4
    (5) 5.5

21. Which of the following expressions would show the area of the basketball court?

    (1) 94 + 50
    (2) 94 x 50
    (3) 2 x 94 x 50
    (4) 2(94) + 2(50)
    (5) 2(94) x 2(50)

22. Morgan works h hours per day. He spends one hour a day traveling between his home and work. He's gone from his home for work and travel a total of 48 hours a week. If he works 4 days a week, which of the following equations would be used to find how many hours a day he works?

    (1) $h + 1 + 4 = 48$
    (2) $4h + 1 = 48$
    (3) $4 - (h + 1) = 48$
    (4) $4(h + 1) = 48$
    (5) $4(h - 1) = 48$

23. Henrietta picked $4\frac{1}{2}$ quarts of strawberries. If she freezes these in six equal packages, how many quarts will be in each package?

    (1) $\frac{1}{3}$
    (2) $\frac{3}{4}$
    (3) $1\frac{1}{2}$
    (4) 27
    (5) Insufficient data is given to solve the problem.

Item 24 is based on the following number line.

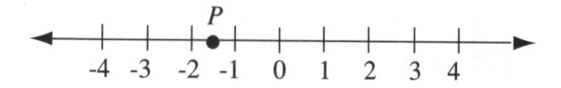

24. What is the value of point P?

    (1) $\frac{1}{2}$
    (2) $1\frac{1}{2}$
    (3) $-1\frac{1}{2}$
    (4) $2\frac{1}{2}$
    (5) $-2\frac{1}{2}$

Items 25 and 26 are based on the following graph.

U.S. GOVERNMENT INCOME

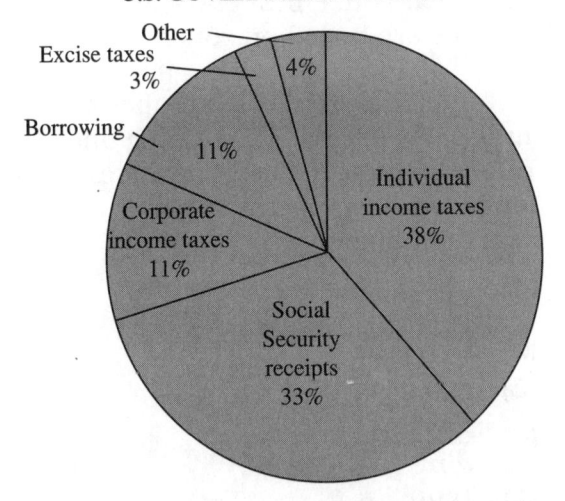

- Other 4%
- Excise taxes 3%
- Borrowing 11%
- Corporate income taxes 11%
- Social Security receipts 33%
- Individual income taxes 38%

25. How much more money does the government receive from individual income taxes and excise taxes than from corporate income taxes?

(1) 8%
(2) 11%
(3) 27%
(4) 30%
(5) 41%

26. If the government received $991 billion in one year, which of the following expressions would show how many billion dollars were from Social Security receipts?

(1) 33 × 991
(2) $\frac{991}{33}$
(3) $\frac{33 \times 991}{100}$
(4) $\frac{33 \times 100}{991}$
(5) $\frac{991 \times 100}{33}$

27. The combined ages of three brothers equals 24. The oldest brother is 10 years older than the youngest brother. What is the age of the youngest brother?

(1) 2
(2) 4
(3) 7
(4) 14
(5) Insufficient data is given to solve the problem.

28. Sharon's weekly salary is $366.80. If she works 40 hours per week, what is her hourly rate of pay?

(1) $ 3.24
(2) $ 3.66
(3) $ 8.24
(4) $ 9.17
(5) $14.64

Item 29 is based on the following figure.

29. What is the measure of angle B?

LEAN-TO CAMPING SHELTER

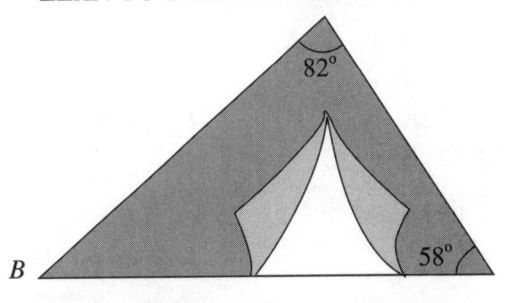

(angles shown: 82°, 58°, vertex B)

(1) 32°
(2) 40°
(3) 82°
(4) 98°
(5) 122°

30. Which of the following values is part of the solution set to $\frac{1}{2}s + 1 > 13$?

(1) 6
(2) 7
(3) 23
(4) 24
(5) 25

31. Jordan bought a box of 25 candy bars that weighed 30 ounces. What was the weight in ounces of each candy bar?

(1) $\frac{1}{5}$
(2) $\frac{1}{6}$
(3) $\frac{5}{6}$

Full-Length Practice Test   79

(4) $1\frac{1}{6}$

(5) $1\frac{1}{5}$

Item 32 is based on the following chart.

ILLNESSES DURING RECENT FLU OUTBREAK

Factory	Employees	Percent Ill
A	100	20%
B	300	18%
C	50	24%
D	125	28%
E	700	6%

32. Which of the following sequences shows the correct order of factories ranked from least to greatest number of employees ill?

   (1) A, B, C, D, E
   (2) B, D, E, C, A
   (3) C, D, A, B, E
   (4) C, A, D, E, B
   (5) D, E, C, B, A

Item 33 is based on the following figure.

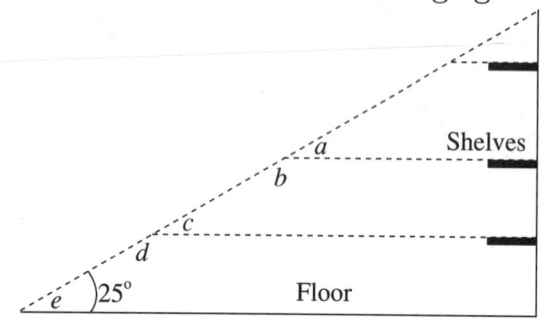

33. If all the shelves are parallel to the floor, what is the measure of angle b in degrees?

   (1) 25
   (2) 50
   (3) 65
   (4) 155
   (5) Insufficient data is given to solve the problem.

Items 34 and 35 are based on the following information.

The cost of sending a first-class letter in 1992 was $0.29 for the first ounce and $0.23 for each additional ounce. Items sent first class had to weigh 11 ounces or less. Any item weighing over that amount had to be sent by priority mail, which is like first class except that rates are based on zones.

34. Irving paid p to mail a number of first-class letters all weighing one ounce. Which of the following expressions would show the number of letters he mailed?

   (1) $\dfrac{p}{\$0.29}$
   (2) $p - \$0.29$
   (3) $p(\$0.29)$
   (4) $\dfrac{\$0.29}{p}$
   (5) $\$0.29 - p$

35. Which of the following expressions would show the cost of postage for a letter weighing q ounces?

   (1) $q(\$0.23 + \$0.29)$
   (2) $\$0.23q + \$0.29$
   (3) $\$0.23(q + 1) + \$0.29$
   (4) $\$0.23\,(q - 1) + \$0.29$
   (5) $(q - 1)(\$0.23 + \$0.29)$

36. The square root of 54 is between which two numbers?

   (1) 4 and 5
   (2) 5 and 6
   (3) 6 and 7
   (4) 7 and 8
   (5) 8 and 9

37. Milton and Victoria left their house at the same time. Milton rode the bus traveling south at 30 miles per hour for $\frac{1}{4}$ hour. Victoria rode the train traveling north at 40 miles per hour for $\frac{3}{4}$ hour. Which of the following expressions would show how many miles apart they are?

   (1) $\left(40 \times \tfrac{3}{4}\right) + \left(30 \times \tfrac{1}{4}\right)$

   (2) $\left(40 \times \tfrac{3}{4}\right) - \left(30 \times \tfrac{1}{4}\right)$

(3) $(40 \times \frac{4}{3}) + (30 \times 4)$

(4) $(30 \times 4) - (40 \times \frac{4}{3})$

(5) $(30 \times \frac{1}{4}) - (40 \times \frac{3}{4})$

38. A real estate developer built eight buildings each with eight apartments in each of eight cities in each of eight states. Each apartment can accommodate up to eight people. Which of the following expressions shows the number of apartments the developer built?

    (1) 8^1
    (2) 8^2
    (3) 8^3
    (4) 8^4
    (5) 8^5

39. Twice as many people work in the stock department as work in the receiving department of a warehouse. Five more people work in the shipping department as work in the stock department. If 145 people work in these departments, which of the following equations could you solve to find how many people work in the receiving department?

    (1) $x + 2x + 5 = 145$
    (2) $x + 2x + x + 5 = \frac{145}{3}$
    (3) $x + 2x + x + 5 = 145$
    (4) $x + 2x + 2x + 5 = 145$
    (5) $x + 2x + 2x + 5 = 3 \times 145$

Items 40 and 41 are based on the following graph.

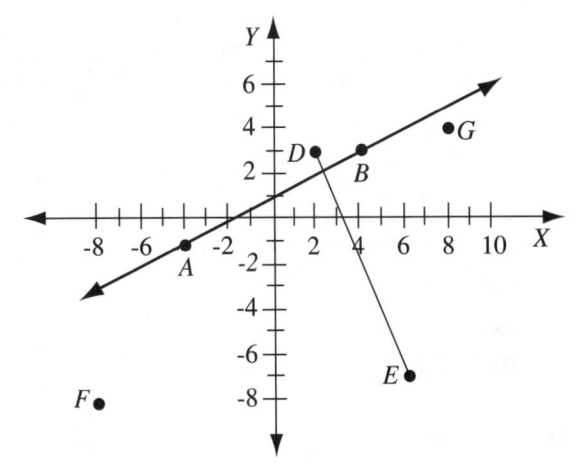

40. What is the slope of line *AB*?

    (1) 0
    (2) $\frac{1}{4}$
    (3) $\frac{1}{2}$
    (4) 1
    (5) 2

41. Using the formula for midpoint, $M = \left(\frac{x_1 + x_2}{2}, \frac{y_1 + y_2}{2} \right)$, what is the midpoint of segment *DE*?

    (1) (4, 4)
    (2) (4, -2)
    (3) (-4, 4)
    (4) (4, 0)
    (5) (0, 4)

Item 42 is based on the following figure.

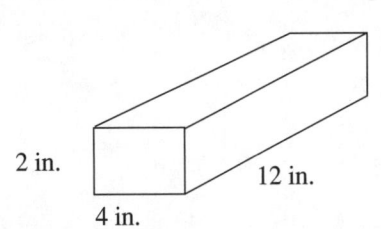

42. Which of the following expressions shows the volume of this box in cubic inches?

    (1) $12 + 4 + 2$
    (2) $12 \times 4 \times 2$
    (3) $12^2 + 4^2 + 2^2$

Full-Length Practice Test   81

(4) 2(12 + 4 + 2)
(5) 2(12) + 2(4) + 2(2)

43. Penelope ordered a book by mail. The total cost was $10.69, including $1.85 postage and 4% sales tax. What was the cost of the book?

(1) $ 7.00
(2) $ 8.35
(3) $ 8.50
(4) $ 8.84
(5) $11.88

44. Factor $e^2 + 7e - 18$.

(1) $(e - 2)(e + 9)$
(2) $(e + 2)(e + 9)$
(3) $(e - 2)(e - 9)$
(4) $(e - 3)(e + 6)$
(5) $(e + 3)(e - 6)$

Item 45 is based on the following figures.

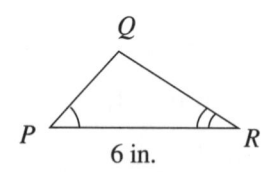

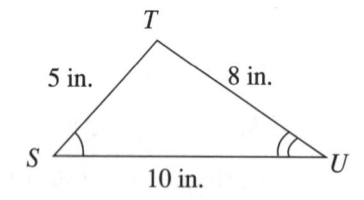

45. Which of the following expressions would show the length of QR in inches?

(1) $\dfrac{6 \times 10}{5}$
(2) $\dfrac{8 \times 10}{6}$
(3) $\dfrac{6 \times 10}{8}$
(4) $\dfrac{6 \times 5}{10}$
(5) $\dfrac{6 \times 8}{10}$

46. Karen, Rick, and Joe sell computers. During a year Karen sold three times as many computers as Rick, and Joe sold eight more than Karen. Together they sold 4194 computers. How many did Joe sell?

(1) 606
(2) 1134
(3) 1647
(4) 1802
(5) Insufficient data is given to solve the problem.

47. Trent bought a new stereo on sale for $539. Its normal cost was $980. What percent of its normal cost did he save?

(1) 27%
(2) 36%
(3) 45%
(4) 54%
(5) 81%

48. Simplify $\dfrac{126 b^{18} c^8}{9 b^{12} c^7}$.

(1) $7b^2c^2$
(2) $14b^6c$
(3) $28b^6c^{15}$
(4) $63b^9c^4$
(5) $117b^6c^{15}$

Item 49 is based on the following figure.

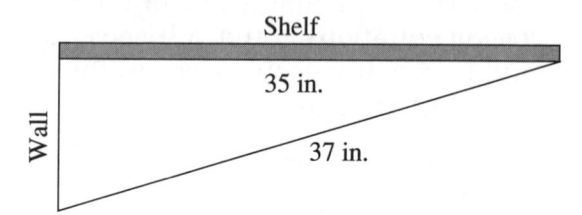

49. Which of the following expressions would show how many inches the distance is from where the shelf meets the wall to where the support meets the wall?

(1) $\sqrt{37 - 35}$
(2) $\sqrt{37 + 35}$
(3) $\sqrt{(37 - 35)^2}$
(4) $\sqrt{37^2 - 35^2}$
(5) $\sqrt{37^2 + 35^2}$

Items 50 and 51 are based on the following graph.

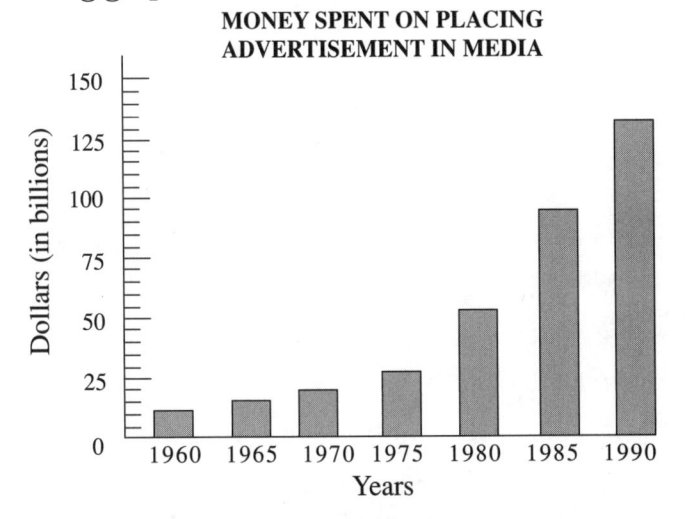

MONEY SPENT ON PLACING ADVERTISEMENT IN MEDIA

50. Approximately how many more dollars were spent on advertising in 1990 than in 1985?

    (1) $ 25 billion
    (2) $ 35 billion
    (3) $ 75 billion
    (4) $130 billion
    (5) $225 billion

51. Approximately how many times more dollars were spent on advertising in 1985 than in 1975?

    (1) 2
    (2) 3
    (3) 4
    (4) 40
    (5) 65

52. During one 8-hour period, Pam was able to assemble six chairs. If she is able to work at that rate throughout a 36-hour workweek, how many chairs would she be able to assemble during that week?

    (1) 24
    (2) 27
    (3) 30
    (4) 34
    (5) 48

Item 53 is based on the following figure.

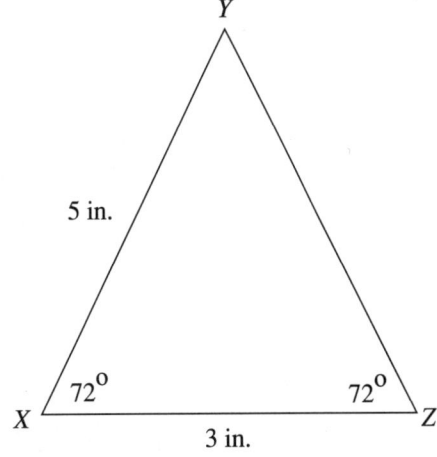

53. What is the perimeter in inches of this triangle?

    (1) 8
    (2) 11
    (3) 13
    (4) 16
    (5) Insufficient data is given to solve the problem.

54. If $w^2 + 2w - 48 = 0$, find the value of w.

    (1) 6 only
    (2) -6 only
    (3) -6 or -8
    (4) 6 or -8
    (5) 8 or -8

55. A jacket regularly priced at $140 is on sale for 20% off. What is the sale price of the jacket?

    (1) $ 28
    (2) $112
    (3) $120
    (4) $168
    (5) Insufficient data is given to solve the problem.

56. Myron bought a carpet measuring five yards by seven yards. If it cost $12 per square yard, what was the carpet's total cost?

    (1) $84

Full-Length Practice Test   83

- **(2)** $144
- **(3)** $288
- **(4)** $420
- **(5)** Insufficient data is given to solve the problem.

Check your answers starting on page 131.

Full-Length Practice Test

Performance Analysis Chart

DIRECTIONS:

Circle the number of each item that you got correct on the Full-Length Practice Test. Count how many items you got correct in each row; count how many items you got correct in each column. Write the number correct per row and column as the numerator in the fraction in the appropriate "Total Correct" box. (The denominators represent the total number of items in the row or column.) Write the grand total correct over the denominator **56** at the lower right corner of the chart. (For example, if you got 50 items correct, write **50** so that the fraction reads **50/56**.) Item numbers in boldface represent items based on graphic material.

Item Type	Arithmetic (Chapters 1-5)	Algebra (Chapters 6)	Geometry (Chapters 7)	Total Correct
Skills	19	5, 17, **24**, 48	**15, 29, 33, 53**	—/9
Application	1, 2, 3, **6**, 7, 9, 11, 13, 14, 16, **20, 21**, 23, **25, 26**, 28, 31, 36, 38, **42, 50, 51**, 52	10, 30, 44, 54	8, **40, 41**, 45	—/31
Problem Solving	4, 32, 37, 47, 55, 56	22, 27, 34, 35, 39, 43, 46	**12, 18, 49**	—/16
Total Correct	—/30	—/15	—/11	—/56

The chapters named in parentheses indicate where in the math instruction of *The Cambridge Comprehensive Program* and *The Cambridge Program for the Mathematics Test* you can find specific instruction about the various areas of mathematics.

On the chart, items are classified as Skills, Application, or Problem Solving. In the mathematics instruction chapters of both textbooks, the three problem types are covered in different levels:

Skills items are covered in Level 1.

Application items are covered in Level 2.

Problem Solving items are covered in Level 3.

For example, the skills needed to solve item 30 are covered in Level 2 of Chapter 6. To locate the chapters in which arithmetic items are addressed, reread the problem to see what kind of numbers (whole numbers, fractions, etc.) are used, and then go to the designated level of the appropriate chapter.

Full-Length Practice Test   85

Simulated Test

TIME: *90 minutes*
DIRECTIONS:
Choose the one best answer for each item.

1. In 1980 a solar-powered airplane was flown from France to England. This flight took 5 hours and 30 minutes at an average speed of 30 miles per hour. What distance in miles did it cover?

    (1) 165
    (2) 176
    (3) 330
    (4) 660
    (5) 900

2. A cheetah can run at a speed of 70 miles per hour. A zebra can run at a speed of 40 miles per hour. Which of the following expressions would give the difference between the distance a cheetah and a zebra can cover in 15 minutes?

    (1) $15(70) - 15(40)$
    (2) $4(70) - 4(40)$
    (3) $\frac{70}{15} - \frac{40}{15}$
    (4) $\frac{70}{4} - \frac{40}{4}$
    (5) $\frac{4}{70} - \frac{4}{40}$

Items 3 to 5 are based on the following information.

Due to a change in the federal income tax laws, home equity loans are becoming popular. Home equity is the difference between the value of a home and the amount owed on it. A home equity loan is based on that amount.

After the tax laws were changed, interest paid for consumer loans, such as car loans, was no longer deductible on income taxes, but interest for home loans remained deductible. By borrowing on the value of a home, some money can be saved on income taxes.

3. Brenda gets a home equity loan for $3000 at 9% for 9 months. How much interest must she pay?

    (1) $180
    (2) $202.50
    (3) $270
    (4) $607.50
    (5) Insufficient data is given to solve the problem.

4. Jack and Samantha want to borrow on their home equity for home improvements. If their home is worth $65,000 and they owe $50,000 on it, how much interest will they pay if they take out a home equity loan at 7% for 5 years?

    (1) $ 1050
    (2) $ 2143
    (3) $ 5250
    (4) $17,500
    (5) Insufficient data is given to solve the problem.

5. Although home equity loans are popular, conventional loans might be cheaper in the long run. What percent lower would the interest rate on a loan of $5000 be if the interest paid on a conventional loan would total $670?

    (1) 8%
    (2) 12%
    (3) 13%
    (4) 22%
    (5) Insufficient data is given to solve the problem.

Simulated Test 87

Item 6 is based on the following figure.

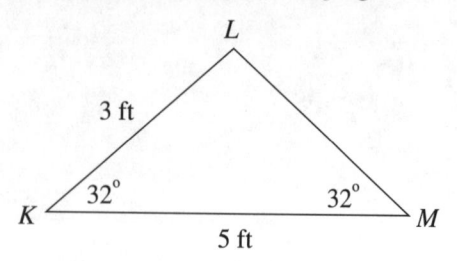

6. What is the perimeter in feet of triangle *KLM*?
   - (1) 8
   - (2) 11
   - (3) 13
   - (4) 15
   - (5) Insufficient data is given to solve the problem.

7. Frank spent $5.60 for eight pads costing *p*. What is the value of *p*?
   - (1) $ 0.70
   - (2) $ 7.00
   - (3) $ 3.60
   - (4) $13.60
   - (5) $44.80

8. Joe bought six hamburgers and four drinks for his family. If the hamburgers cost $2.50 each and the drinks cost $1 each, what was the total cost?
   - (1) $10
   - (2) $15
   - (3) $19
   - (4) $21
   - (5) $35

9. If it takes Bill Tribbon 2.8 hours to build a bookcase, how many hours will it take him to build 14 of them?
   - (1) 2
   - (2) 16.8
   - (3) 20
   - (4) 39.2
   - (5) Insufficient data is given to solve the problem.

10. The Flidget Company has 68 employees and a weekly payroll of $23,596. What is the average salary there?
    - (1) $235
    - (2) $337
    - (3) $347
    - (4) $393
    - (5) $414

Item 11 is based on the following figure.

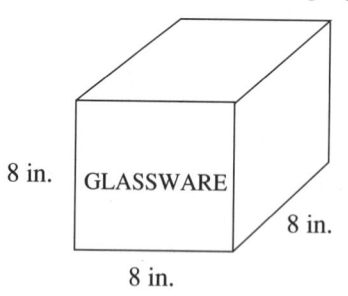

11. What is the volume of the box in cubic inches?
    - (1) 24
    - (2) 48
    - (3) 64
    - (4) 256
    - (5) 512

Item 12 is based on the following figure.

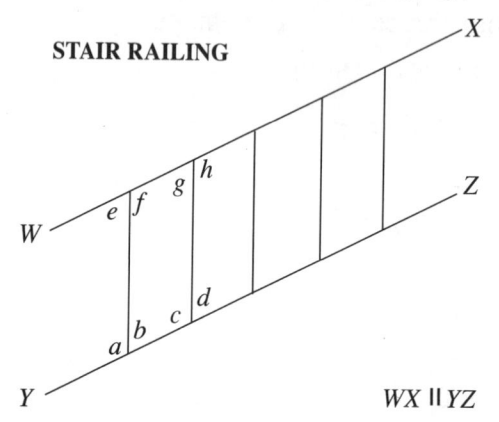

WX ∥ YZ

12. The measure of angle *a* is 116°. What is the measure of angle *g*?
    - (1) 26°
    - (2) 64°
    - (3) 84°
    - (4) 116°
    - (5) Insufficient data is given to solve the problem.

Item 13 is based on the following figure.

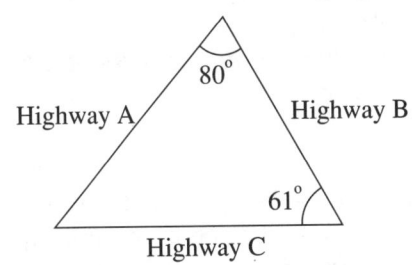

13. Which of the highway segments shown is the longest?

    (1) Highway A
    (2) Highway B
    (3) Highway C
    (4) Highways A and B are equal.
    (5) Insufficient data is given to solve the problem.

14. What is the value of $x^2 - 11x - 24$ if $x = -3$?

    (1) -9
    (2) 15
    (3) -18
    (4) 18
    (5) -48

15. Raul sent 8 packages each weighing 4 pounds 4 ounces. If it cost him $0.40 per pound to mail them, what was his total cost?

    (1) $ 1.70
    (2) $ 3.20
    (3) $12.80
    (4) $13.60
    (5) $51.20

16. A subscription to a weekly magazine costs $59.80 per year. What is the price of a single issue?

    (1) $0.60
    (2) $1.15
    (3) $2.30
    (4) $3.10
    (5) Insufficient data is given to solve the problem.

Item 17 is based on the following graph.

U.S. POPULATION

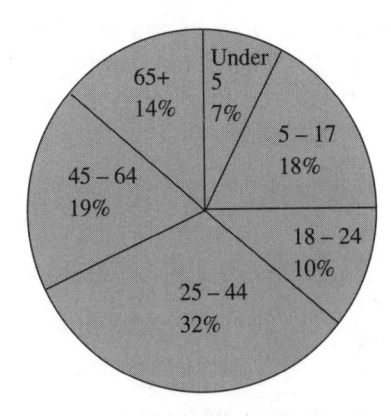

17. How much more of the population is adult (18 to 64) than child (under 18) or senior citizen (over 64)?

    (1) 11%
    (2) 22%
    (3) 39%
    (4) 40%
    (5) 61%

18. A charity planned to sell 500 raffle tickets. When each ticket was sold, one part of the ticket was given to the buyer, and the other part was placed in a bowl for the grand prize drawing. All but 30 tickets were sold. If Gary bought two tickets, which of the following expressions represents the probability of his winning the grand prize?

    (1) $\dfrac{1}{30}$
    (2) $\dfrac{1}{500-30}$
    (3) $\dfrac{2}{500}$
    (4) $\dfrac{2}{500-30}$
    (5) $\dfrac{2}{500+30}$

19. Simplify $7m - 3n + 10n - 9m$.

    (1) $-2m - 7n$
    (2) $-2m + 7n$
    (3) $2m + 13n$

(4) $4m + n$
(5) $5mn$

20. It takes Milo 40 minutes to drive to work, a distance of 15 miles. What is Milo's average speed in miles per hour during his drive to work?

    (1) $22\frac{1}{2}$
    (2) 25
    (3) $26\frac{2}{3}$
    (4) 55
    (5) 60

21. Ron is a salesperson at a music store. In one week he sold $3000 in tapes and compact discs. If all but 15% of his sales were to repeat customers, which expression would show how much he sold to new customers?

    (1) $p = \$3000 \times 15$
    (2) $p = \$3000(100 - 15)$
    (3) $p = \dfrac{\$3000 \times 15}{100}$
    (4) $p = \dfrac{\$3000(100 - 15)}{100}$
    (5) $p = \dfrac{\$3000}{100 - 15}$

22. Bobbie charged a total of $148.95 during a shopping trip. If one purchase cost $37.63, which of the following equations would give the amount of the remaining purchases? (Use x to show the remaining purchases.)

    (1) $x - \$37.63 = \$148.95$
    (2) $\$37.63x = \$148.95$
    (3) $\$37.63 - x = \$148.95$
    (4) $\$37.63 + x = \$148.95$
    (5) $\dfrac{\$37.63}{x} = \$148.95$

23. Brett made a circular flower bed that has an area of 153.86 square feet. What is the radius in feet of this flower bed?

    (1) 7
    (2) 12
    (3) 21
    (4) 49
    (5) Insufficient data is given to solve the problem.

24. Leonard bought four pairs of socks each costing x. With 4% sales tax he paid a total of $8.52. Which of the following equations would give the price of a single pair of socks?

    (1) $4x + 0.04 = \$8.52$
    (2) $4(x + 0.04) = \$8.52$
    (3) $4(0.04x) = \$8.52$
    (4) $0.04(4x) = \$8.52$
    (5) $4x + 0.04(4x) = \$8.52$

Item 25 is based on the following number line.

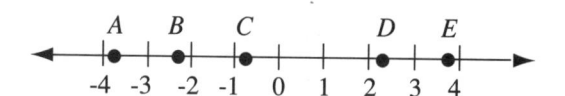

25. Which point corresponds to the point $-3\frac{3}{4}$?

    (1) A
    (2) B
    (3) C
    (4) D
    (5) E

Item 26 is based on the following figure.

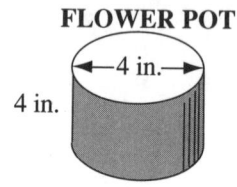

FLOWER POT

26. In cubic inches, what is the volume of the flowerpot?

    (1) 25.12
    (2) 50.24
    (3) 75.36
    (4) 150.72
    (5) 200.96

27. For $135 Ben can buy a new car battery and two tires. If the battery costs $57, which of the following expressions could

be solved to find the price of a single tire, t?

(1) $t + \$57 = \$135$
(2) $2t - \$57 = \$135$
(3) $2t + \$57 = \$135$
(4) $\dfrac{t}{2} - \$57 = \$135$
(5) $\dfrac{t}{2} + \$57 = \$135$

28. Ben and Roger work at the same company. Ben has worked there 3 years less than twice as long as Roger. Together they have worked there a total of 54 years. How many years has Ben worked at the company?

(1) 19
(2) 35
(3) 38
(4) 41
(5) 57

29. The cost of 5 tickets to a football game plus $8 is the same as 9 tickets to the game minus $28. How much does a ticket cost?

(1) $ 3
(2) $ 4
(3) $ 9
(4) $12
(5) $13

30. What is the correct order from largest to smallest fraction of maximum capacity for the following events?

Event	Attendance	Capacity
A. Basketball Game	1400	2100
B. Play	180	200
C. Concert	18	36
D. Lecture	8	20
E. Dance	100	120

(1) A, B, E, C, D
(2) B, E, A, C, D
(3) B, E, D, A, C
(4) C, A, D, E, B
(5) D, C, A, E, B

31. Beth drove 30 miles north from Blue Ridge to Greentown. Then she drove 25 miles west to Red Rock. Which of the following expresses the straight-line distance from Blue Ridge to Red Rock?

(1) $c = \sqrt{30 + 25}$
(2) $c = \sqrt{(30 + 25)^2}$
(3) $c = \sqrt{30^2 + 25^2}$
(4) $c = \sqrt{(30 - 25)^2}$
(5) $c = \sqrt{30^2 - 25^2}$

Item 32 is based on the following figure.

32. The hardcover book is published in a softcover edition similar in size but only five inches long. Which of the following expresses the width in inches of the softcover book?

(1) $\dfrac{12 \times 8}{5}$
(2) $\dfrac{12 - 8}{5}$
(3) $\dfrac{12 \times 5}{8}$
(4) $\dfrac{12 - 5}{8}$
(5) $\dfrac{8 \times 5}{12}$

33. Which of the following values is part of the solution set of $\tfrac{1}{3}h - 2 \geq 7$?

(1) 3
(2) 5
(3) 9
(4) 25
(5) 27

Item 34 is based on the following graph.

CONSUMER PRICE INDEX

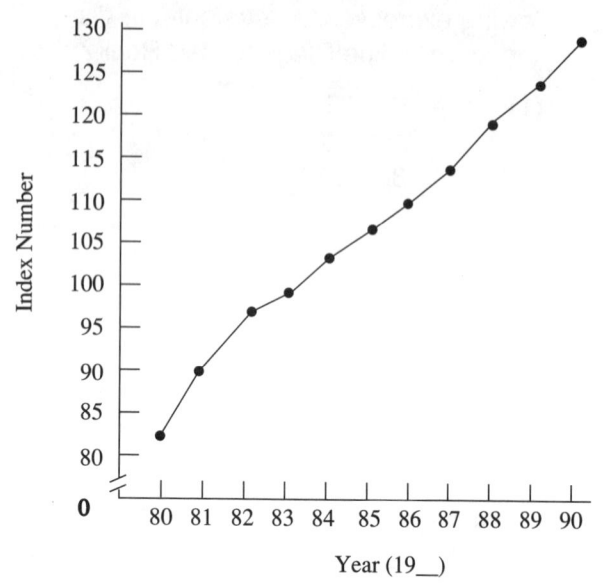

[Graph showing Index Number vs Year (19__), with points rising from about 82 in 1980 to about 128 in 1990]

34. By approximately how much did the Consumer Price Index increase from 1985 to 1989?

(1) 3
(2) 4
(3) 17
(4) 22
(5) 25

Item 35 is based on the following figure.

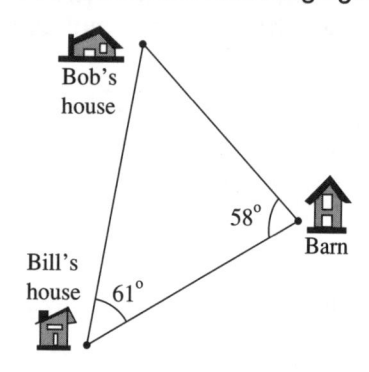

[Triangle diagram with Bob's house at top, Bill's house at bottom left (61°), and Barn at right (58°)]

35. According to the diagram, which of the following statements is true?

(1) Both houses are the same distance from the barn.
(2) Bill's house is closer to the barn than Bob's house.
(3) Bob's house is closer to the barn than Bill's house.
(4) The barn is closer to Bob's house than Bill's.
(5) Insufficient data is given to solve the problem.

Item 36 is based on the following figure.

ROOF SUPPORT

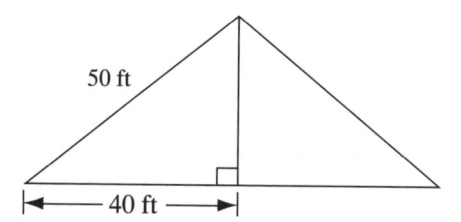

[Triangle with slant side 50 ft and half-base 40 ft, with right angle at center]

36. How many feet high is the middle suspension support?

(1) 20
(2) 25
(3) 30
(4) 40
(5) 80

37. Herman works for a soft drink company, setting up displays in stores. If he sets up a display of 12-can packages of soft drinks that has a 12-package base and is stacked 12 packages high in 12 different stores, which of the following expressions shows how many cans he used?

(1) 12^1
(2) 12^2
(3) 12^3
(4) 12^4
(5) 12^5

38. The diameter of the sun is estimated to be 8.654×10^5 miles. Which of the following numbers is equal to that amount?

(1) 8,650
(2) 86,540
(3) 865,400
(4) 8,654,000
(5) 86,540,000

39. Vincent owns $5\frac{5}{8}$ acres of land. He plans to divide it equally among his six grand-

Simulated Test

children. How much land in acres will each grandchild receive?

(1) $\frac{3}{8}$
(2) $\frac{5}{16}$
(3) $\frac{1}{2}$
(4) $\frac{9}{16}$
(5) $\frac{15}{16}$

40. What was Dora's average daily calorie intake for the week?

Day	Calories
Sunday	1050
Monday	1100
Tuesday	1230
Wednesday	980
Thursday	950
Friday	1100
Saturday	1290

(1) 900
(2) 1000
(3) 1050
(4) 1100
(5) 1200

41. Barbie bought five tickets in a raffle. If there were 28,000 tickets sold, what are her chances of winning a prize?

(1) $\frac{1}{28}$
(2) $\frac{1}{56}$
(3) $\frac{1}{5600}$
(4) $\frac{1}{28,000}$
(5) Insufficient data is given to solve the problem.

Items 42 and 43 are based on the following graph.

WORLD'S BUSIEST AIRPORTS, 1988

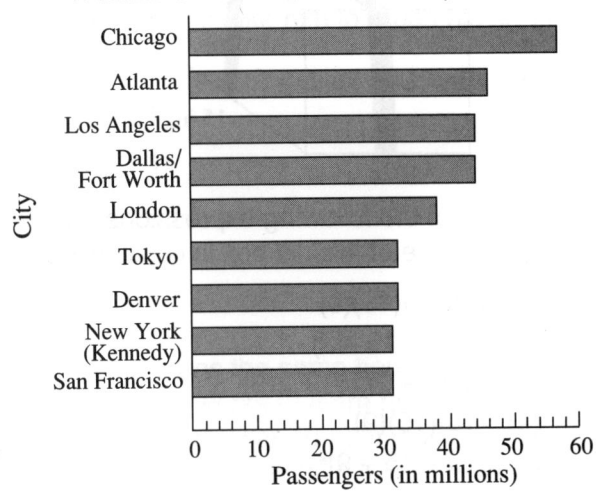

42. The Denver airport is called a "hub" airport because many airlines fly their passengers there to get connecting flights to their final destination. If 65% of the Denver passengers were flown there because it is a hub, for how many million passengers was Denver the final destination?

(1) 11.2
(2) 19.5
(3) 20.8
(4) 26.0
(5) Insufficient data is given to solve the problem.

43. Which of the following airport passenger ratios is 3:2?

(1) Tokyo to Atlanta
(2) Chicago to London
(3) Chicago to Los Angeles
(4) London to Tokyo
(5) Insufficient data is given to solve the problem.

Simulated Test

Performance Analysis Chart

DIRECTIONS:

Circle the number of each item that you got correct on the Simulated Test. Count how many items you got correct in each row; count how many items you got correct in each column. Write the number correct per row and column as the numerator in the fraction in the appropriate "Total Correct" box. (The denominators represent the total number of items in the row or column.) Write the grand total correct over the denominator **56** at the lower right corner of the chart. (For example, if you got 50 items correct, write **50** so that the fraction reads **50/56**.) Item numbers in boldface represent items based on graphic material.

Item Type	Arithmetic (Chapters 1-5)	Algebra (Chapter 6)	Geometry (Chapter 7)	Total Correct
Skills		14, 19, **25**, 51	**6, 12, 13, 35**	—/8
Application	1, 3, 9, 10, **11**, 15, 16, **17**, 18, 20, **26**, 30, **34**, 37, 38, 39, 40, 41, **42, 43, 44**, 48, 55	33, 50	**32, 46, 47**, 49	—/29
Problem Solving	2, 4, 5, 8, 21, 52, 53, 54	7, 22, 24, 27, 28, 29, 45, 56	23, 31, **36**	—/19
Total Correct	—/31	—/14	—/11	—/56

The chapters named in parentheses indicate where in the math instruction of *The Cambridge Comprehensive Program* and *The Cambridge Program for the Mathematics Test* you can find specific instruction about the various areas of mathematics.

On the chart, items are classified as Skills, Application, or Problem Solving. In the mathematics instruction chapters of both textbooks, the three problem types are covered in different levels:

Skills items are covered in Level 1.
Application items are covered in Level 2.
Problem Solving items are covered in Level 3.

For example, the skills needed to solve item 33 are covered in Level 2 of Chapter 6. To locate the chapters in which arithmetic items are addressed, reread the problem to see what kind of numbers (whole numbers, fractions, etc.) are used, and then go to the designated level of the appropriate chapter.

96 Simulated Test

Answers and Explanations

Chapter 1: Whole Numbers

Level 1

1. 5

2. 4

3. 700

4. 6,000,000

5. 90,000

6.
```
      59
   ×  47
     413
     236
    2773
```

7.
```
   6003
 −  926
   5077
```

8.
```
      24
   21)504
      42
      ──
       84
       84
       ──
        0
```

9.
```
   15,800
 −  4,932
   10,868
```

10.
```
        2 r 203
   429)1061
       858
       ───
       203
```

11.
```
     364
     855
      32
   + 678
    1929
```

12.
```
     3807
  ×    72
     7614
    26649
   274,104
```

13.
```
       86
    9,440
      302
 + 51,394
   61,222
```

14.
```
       184
   32)5888
      32
      ──
      268
      256
      ───
       128
       128
       ───
         0
```

15.
```
   52,004
 − 43,997
    8,007
```

16.
```
      974
   ×  639
     8766
     2922
     5844
   622,386
```

17. (4)
```
   9614
 −  439
```

18. (2)
```
    382
 ×   61
```

19. (4) 85)3060

20. (3)
```
      96
     704
   +   8
```

Level 2

1. **25,000** The digit 4 is in the thousands place. The digit to the right of 4 is 6, which is more than 4. Add 1 to the thousands digit and put zeros to the right.

2. **$6,700,000** The digit 7 is in the hundred-thousands place. The digit to the right of 7 is 4, which is less than 5. Leave 7 as it is and put zeros to the right.

21. **(1)**
$$52\overline{)\begin{array}{r}\$35\\ \$1820\end{array}}$$
$$\underline{156}$$
$$260$$
$$\underline{260}$$
$$0$$

22. **(4)** $V = lwh$
    $V = 2 \times 2 \times 3$
    $V = \mathbf{12\ ft^3}$

23. **(4)** Round $7894 to $8000.
    Round $1052 to $1000.
    $8000 + $1000 = **$9000**

24. **(1)** Round 26,245 to 26,000.
    Round 43,478 to 43,000.
    43,000 − 26,000 = **17,000**

25. **(3)** Round 325 to 300.
    Round 17 to 20.
    300 × 20 = **6000**

26. **(4)** 15 × 18 = 270
    12 × 25 = 300
    300 − 270 = **30 mi**

27. **(3)** Find the total wages and total number of employees:
    2 × $6 = $12
    6 × $8 = $48
    4 × $12 = $48
    Total wages:
    $12 + $48 + $48 = $108
    Total employees:
    2 + 6 + 4 = 12
    Average wage:
    $$12\overline{)\begin{array}{r}\$9\\ \$108\end{array}}$$
    $$\underline{108}$$
    $$0$$

28. **(2)** Total number of chairs:
    29 × 15 = 435
    Find the difference between chairs and attendance:
    435 − 296 = **139**

29. **(3)** Area of walk:
    3 × 5 = 15
    Area of patio:
    15 × 10 = 150
    Area of walk and patio:
    15 + 150 = **165 ft²**

30. **(5) Friday.** Three days' sales were greater and three days' sales were less than Friday's.

31. **(2)** $678 − $490 = **$188**

32. **(3)** Find the net profit on one mattress:
    $318 − $229 = $89
    8 × $89 = **$712**

33. **(2)** Find the total sales:
    $49 + $87 + $318 + $170 = $624
    $$4\overline{)\begin{array}{r}\$156\\ \$624\end{array}}$$

34. **(4)** 178 − 145

35. **(5)** $\dfrac{498 - 182}{40}$
    Subtract the deductions from the weekly earnings. Then divide by the number of hours she works in a week.

36. **(3) 12(4 × 5).** Multiply the area of the room in square yards by the cost of carpet per square yard.

37. **(3) 685 − (21 + 98 + 66 + 182).** The checks are totaled, and then the total is subtracted from the balance.

38. **(4)** $\dfrac{347{,}984 \times 122}{8876}$
    The number of newspapers times the number of pages gives the total number of pages. Divide that product by the number of pages per roll of newsprint to get the number of rolls used.

39. **(1)** 20(2) + 5(3)
    Price of turkey = 20(2)
    Price of doughnuts = 5(3)
    These two costs are added.

40. **(4) 48(356) + 466.** The total price equals the down payment plus the total monthly payments.

Chapter 2: Decimals

Level 1

1. 9
2. 4
3. Eighty-six thousandths
4. 5.000635
5. Thirty and four hundred seventy-six ten-thousandths
6. 0.09021
7. ```
     5.02
     0.51
   + 0.6
   ─────
     6.13
   ```
8. ```
     11.92
   −  2.455

     11.920
   −  2.455
   ──────
      9.465
   ```
9. 0.0462
   ```
         0.105
   ×      0.44
   ──────────
           420
           420
   ──────────
       0.04620
   ```
   Drop the final zero.
10. ```
         0.00337
       ┌────────
     3 )0.01011
         9
         ──
         11
          9
         ──
         21
         21
         ──
          0
   ```
11. ```
              500
         ┌──────         ┌──────
    0.11 )55      =  11 )5500
                        55
                        ──
                        000
   ```
12. ```
                9.08
         ┌────────         ┌────────
    0.06 )0.5448    =   6 )54.48
                        54
                        ──
                         04
                          0
                         ──
                         48
                         48
                         ──
                          0
   ```
13. ```
      11.876
       5
   +   5.3
   ───────
      22.176
   ```
14. ```
       12.5
   ×   0.08
   ───────
      1.000 = 1
   ```
15. ```
         3            3.000
   −  0.019      −    0.019
                   ──────────
                       2.981
   ```
16. ```
                   325
        ┌─────           ┌─────────
   0.64)208   = 64)20,800
                       19 2
                       ────
                        1 60
                        1 28
                        ────
                         320
                         320
                         ────
                           0
   ```
17. ```
                     1.3
        ┌────────         ┌──────
  0.012 )0.0156   = 12 )15.6
                        12
                        ──
                        36
                        36
                        ──
                         0
   ```
18. **0.03**   0.03 = 0.030
    0.014 = 0.014
    0.030 is larger than 0.014.
19. **0.027, 0.2, 0.207, 0.27**
    0.27 = 0.270
    0.027 = 0.027
    0.207 = 0.207
    0.2 = 0.200
20. **8.405, 8.4, 8.05, 8.045**
    8.4 = 8.400
    8.045 = 8.045
    8.405 = 8.405
    8.05 = 8.050

23. (4) Babies born in 1990:
 $16.7 \times 23 = 384.1$
 Babies born in 1980:
 $15.9 \times 19 = 302.1$
 $384.1 - 302.1 = $ **82**

24. (5) The rate decreased and then gradually increased.

25. (5) $4.3 \times 30 = $ **129 mi**

26. (3)
$$8.8 \overline{)184.8} = 88 \overline{)1848}\frac{21 \text{ gal}}{}$$
$$\phantom{8.8 \overline{)184.8} = 88)}\underline{176}$$
$$\phantom{8.8 \overline{)184.8} = 88)00}88$$
$$\phantom{8.8 \overline{)184.8} = 88)00}\underline{88}$$
$$\phantom{8.8 \overline{)184.8} = 88)000}0$$

27. (4) Gallons needed:
 $25.0 - 7.2 = 17.8$
 $\$1.189$
 $\times 17.8$
 $\overline{9512}$
 8323
 1189
 $\overline{\$21.1642}$

 $\$21.1642$ rounds to **$21.16**.

28. (5) $(38.5 \times 10) - (21.7 \times 15)$
 Subtract the total miles an Antelope can travel on a full tank of gas from the total miles a Carp can travel.

29. (3) Ricky: Anne:
 $d = rt$ $d = rt$
 $d = 50 \times 4.75$ $d = 55 \times 7.5$
 $d = 237.5$ mi $d = 412.5$ mi
 $412.5 - 237.5 = $ **175 mi**

30. (5) Eastbound bus: Westbound bus:
 $d = rt$ $d = rt$
 $d = 60 \times 3.5$ $d = 50 \times 3.5$
 $d = 210$ mi $d = 175$ mi
 $210 + 175 = $ **385 mi**

31. (3) First car: Second car:
 $d = rt$ $d = rt$
 $d = 65 \times 1.5$ $d = 60 \times 2.25$
 $d = 97.5$ mi $d = 135$ mi
 $97.5 + 135 = $ **232.5 mi**

32. (4)
$$31.2 \overline{)374} = 312 \overline{)3740.0}\frac{11.9 \text{ gal}}{}$$
$$\phantom{31.2 \overline{)374} = 312)}\underline{312}$$
$$\phantom{31.2 \overline{)374} = 312)0}620$$
$$\phantom{31.2 \overline{)374} = 312)0}\underline{312}$$
$$\phantom{31.2 \overline{)374} = 312)}3080$$
$$\phantom{31.2 \overline{)374} = 312)}\underline{2808}$$
$$\phantom{31.2 \overline{)374} = 312)0}272$$

 11.9 gal rounds to **12 gal.**

33. (3) Regular earnings:
 $40 \times \$8.50 = \$340.00$
 Overtime earnings:
 $8 \times \$12.00 = \$96.00$
 $\$340.00 + \$96.00 = $ **$436.00**

34. (2)
$$6.5 \overline{)\$4.03} = 65 \overline{)\$40.30}\frac{\$0.62}{}$$
$$\phantom{6.5 \overline{)\$4.03} = 65)}390$$
$$\phantom{6.5 \overline{)\$4.03} = 65)}130$$
$$\phantom{6.5 \overline{)\$4.03} = 65)}\underline{130}$$
$$\phantom{6.5 \overline{)\$4.03} = 65)00}0$$

35. (2) Day 1, Day 5, Day 2, Day 4, Day 3

36. (4) $99.8°F + 2.4°F - 1.6°F = $ **100.6°F**

37. (1) The weights of all four packages are given.
 $3.2 + 1.6 + 2.7 + 2.7 = 10.2$
$$4 \overline{)10.20}\frac{2.55 \text{ lb}}{}$$
$$\underline{8}$$
$$22$$
$$\underline{20}$$
$$20$$
$$\underline{20}$$
$$0$$

38. (5) Insufficient data is given to solve the problem. The weight of the chicken is not given.

39. (5) Insufficient data is given to solve the problem. The number of people who work in the office is not given.

40. (3) Mary's rate of speed is not given, but it is not needed to answer the question.
 $d = rt$
 $d = 5.5 \times 65$
 $d = $ **357.5 mi**

Chapter 3: Fractions

Level 1

1. $\frac{8 \div 4}{20 \div 4} = \frac{2}{5}$

2. $16 \overline{)96}$, $\frac{7 \times 6}{16 \times 6} = \frac{42}{96}$
   $\underline{96}$
   0

3. $12 \overline{)62}$ $5\frac{2}{12}$, $5\frac{2 \div 2}{12 \div 2} = \mathbf{5\frac{1}{6}}$
   $\underline{60}$
   2

4. $\frac{56}{13}$
   $4 \times 13 = 52$
   $52 + 4 = 56$

5. $\frac{5 \times 2}{6 \times 2} = \frac{10}{12}$
   $+ \quad \frac{7}{12} = \frac{7}{12}$
   $\overline{\quad\quad\quad \frac{17}{12} = \mathbf{1\frac{5}{12}}}$

6. $\frac{5}{8}$
   $\frac{5 \times 3}{8 \times 3} = \frac{15}{24}$
   $\frac{7 \times 2}{12 \times 2} = \frac{14}{24}$

7. $\quad 6 = 5\frac{9}{9}$
   $- \; 1\frac{8}{9} = 1\frac{8}{9}$
   $\overline{\quad\quad\quad \mathbf{4\frac{1}{9}}}$

8. $\frac{7}{9} \times \frac{3}{8} \times \frac{5}{14} =$
   $\frac{\cancel{7}^1}{\cancel{9}^3} \times \frac{\cancel{3}^1}{8} \times \frac{5}{\cancel{14}^2} = \mathbf{\frac{5}{48}}$

9. $0.075 = \frac{75}{1000} = \mathbf{\frac{3}{40}}$

10. $15 \div 1\frac{1}{5} =$
    $\frac{15}{1} \div \frac{6}{5} = \frac{\cancel{15}^5}{1} \times \frac{5}{\cancel{6}_2} = \frac{25}{2} = \mathbf{12\frac{1}{2}}$

11. $\frac{5}{8} \times 6 = \frac{5}{\cancel{8}_4} \times \frac{\cancel{6}^3}{1} = \frac{15}{4} = \mathbf{3\frac{3}{4}}$

12. $\frac{5}{6}, \frac{4}{9}, \frac{5}{12}, \frac{7}{18}$
    $\frac{4 \times 4}{9 \times 4} = \frac{16}{36}$
    $\frac{5 \times 6}{6 \times 6} = \frac{30}{36}$
    $\frac{5 \times 3}{12 \times 3} = \frac{15}{36}$
    $\frac{7 \times 2}{18 \times 2} = \frac{14}{36}$

13. $7.8 = 7\frac{8}{10} = \mathbf{7\frac{4}{5}}$

14. 0.24
    $25 \overline{)6.00}$
    $\underline{50}$
    100
    $\underline{100}$
    0

15. $5\frac{1}{2} = 5\frac{4}{8} = 4\frac{4}{8} + \frac{8}{8} = 4\frac{12}{8}$
    $- \; 2\frac{5}{8} = 2\frac{5}{8}$
    $\overline{ \mathbf{2\frac{7}{8}}}$

16. $5\frac{1}{4} = 5\frac{3}{12}$
    $1\frac{2}{3} = 1\frac{8}{12}$
    $+ \; \frac{5}{6} = \frac{10}{12}$
    $\overline{ 6\frac{21}{12} = 6 + 1\frac{9}{12} = 7\frac{9 \div 3}{12 \div 3} = \mathbf{7\frac{3}{4}}}$

17. $4\frac{2}{5} = 4\frac{6}{15}$
    $- \; 2\frac{1}{3} = 2\frac{5}{15}$
    $\overline{ \mathbf{2\frac{1}{15}}}$

18. $1\frac{3}{5} \times 4\frac{1}{6} =$
    $\frac{\cancel{8}^4}{5} \times \frac{\cancel{25}^5}{\cancel{6}_3} = \frac{20}{3} = \mathbf{6\frac{2}{3}}$

19. $\frac{8}{21} \div \frac{4}{7} = \frac{\cancel{8}^2}{\cancel{21}_3} \times \frac{\cancel{7}^1}{\cancel{4}_1} = \mathbf{\frac{2}{3}}$

20. $1\frac{1}{2} \div 2\frac{3}{4} =$
    $\frac{3}{2} \div \frac{11}{4} = \frac{3}{\cancel{2}_1} \times \frac{\cancel{4}^2}{11} = \mathbf{\frac{6}{11}}$

Level 2

1. $\frac{\text{employees}}{\text{total}} = \mathbf{\frac{59}{81}}$

2. $\frac{500 \div 500}{2000 \div 500} = \mathbf{\frac{1}{4}}$ t

3. $\mathbf{2}$ **hr 44 min**
   $60 \overline{)164}$
   $\underline{120}$
   44

4. $6 \times 2 = \mathbf{12}$ **pt**

5. $\mathbf{1\frac{3}{8}}$ **in.** A is at the third $\frac{1}{8}$-inch line between 1 and 2 inches.

6. $2\frac{1}{4} = 2\frac{2}{8} = 1\frac{2}{8} + \frac{8}{8} = 1\frac{10}{8}$
   $- \; 1\frac{3}{8} = 1\frac{3}{8}$
   $\overline{ \mathbf{\frac{7}{8}}}$ **in.**

7. $\frac{3}{20} \times \frac{3}{20} = \mathbf{\frac{9}{400}}$

8. $\frac{\sqrt{121}}{\sqrt{169}} = \mathbf{\frac{11}{13}}$

9. $A = \frac{1}{2}bh$
    $A = \frac{1}{2} \times 8 \times 6$
    $A = \frac{1}{\cancel{2}} \times \frac{\cancel{8}^4}{1} \times \frac{6}{1}$
    $A = \mathbf{24 \ in.^2}$

10. $P = 2l + 2w$
    $P = 2 \times 8\frac{1}{2} + 2 \times 11\frac{7}{8}$
    $P = \frac{\cancel{2}^1}{1} \times \frac{17}{\cancel{2}_1} + \frac{\cancel{2}^1}{1} \times \frac{95}{\cancel{8}_4}$
    $P = \frac{17}{1} + \frac{95}{4}$
    $P = 17 + 23\frac{3}{4}$
    $P = \mathbf{40\frac{3}{4} \ ft}$

11. $A = bh$
    $A = 6 \times 1\frac{3}{4}$
    $A = \frac{\cancel{6}^3}{1} \times \frac{7}{\cancel{4}_2}$
    $A = \frac{21}{2}$
    $A = \mathbf{10\frac{1}{2} \ ft^2}$

12. sale price : regular price = 80:130 = **8:13**

13. $\frac{4}{7} = \frac{52}{t}$
    $4t = 364$
    $t = \mathbf{91}$

14. $\frac{3 \div 3}{1800 \div 3} = \frac{1}{600}$

15. $4 + 5 + 2 + 3 - 1 = 13$ total
    $\frac{5}{13}$

16. (2) $72 - 27 = 45$ employees not sick
    $\frac{45 \div 9}{72 \div 9} = \frac{5}{8}$

17. (4) $4\frac{1}{2} \div 3 = \frac{9}{2} \div \frac{3}{1} = \frac{\cancel{9}^3}{2} \times \frac{1}{\cancel{3}_1} = \frac{3}{2} =$
    $\mathbf{1\frac{1}{2} \ yd}$

18. (5) $1\frac{1}{2} \times 60 = \frac{3}{\cancel{2}} \times \frac{\cancel{60}^{30}}{1} = \frac{90}{1} = \mathbf{90 \ sec}$

19. (1) $3\frac{2}{4} = \mathbf{3\frac{1}{2} \ gal}$
    $4\overline{)14}$
    $\ \ \ \underline{12}$
    $\ \ \ \ \ 2$

20. (3) $2\frac{3}{4}$
    D is at the third $\frac{1}{4}$-inch line between 2 and 3 inches.

21. (3) $\ \ \ 2\frac{3}{4} = 2\frac{12}{16}$
    $\ \ -\ \ \frac{7}{16} = \ \ \frac{7}{16}$
    $\ \ \ \ \ \ \ \ \ \ \ \ \ \mathbf{2\frac{5}{16} \ in.}$

22. (1) $\frac{2}{5} \times \frac{2}{5} \times \frac{2}{5} = \frac{8}{125}$

23. $\frac{\sqrt{4}}{\sqrt{9}} = \frac{2}{3}$

24. (3) $P = 4s$
    $P = 4 \times 5\frac{1}{4}$
    $P = \frac{\cancel{4}^1}{1} \times \frac{21}{\cancel{4}_1}$
    $P = \mathbf{21 \ in.}$

25. (3) $A = \frac{1}{2}bh$
    $A = \frac{1}{2} \times 20 \times 9$
    $A = \frac{1}{\cancel{2}} \times \frac{\cancel{20}^{10}}{1} \times \frac{9}{1}$
    $A = \frac{90}{1}$
    $A = \mathbf{90 \ ft^2}$

26. (5) **Insufficient data is given to solve the problem.** The height of the parallelogram is not given.

27. (3) $105 - 25 = 80$ new cars
    used cars:new cars = 25:80 or
    $\frac{25}{80} = \frac{5}{16}$

28. (3) $\frac{3}{10} = \frac{b}{30}$
    $90 = 10b$
    $\mathbf{9} = b$

29. (5) $\frac{6}{3900} = \frac{1}{650}$

30. (5) $\frac{16}{27}$
    $6 + 10 = 16$ sweatshirts and sweatpants
    $6 + 10 + 8 + 3 = 27$ total

Level 3

1. $\frac{\text{peanuts}}{\text{cashews}} \quad \frac{5}{2} = \frac{15}{x}$
    $\ \ \ \ \ \ \ \ \ \ \ \ \ \ \ 5x = 30$
    $\ \ \ \ \ \ \ \ \ \ \ \ \ \ \ \ \ x = \mathbf{6 \ lb}$

2. $\frac{\text{hours}}{\text{earnings}} \quad \frac{6}{\$45.60} = \frac{40}{x}$
    $\ \ \ \ \ \ \ \ \ \ \ \ \ \ \ \ \ \ 6x = \$1824.00$
    $\ x = \mathbf{\$304.00}$

3. $\frac{\text{salaried}}{\text{nonsalaried}} \quad \frac{2}{25} = \frac{x}{375}$
    $\ \ \ \ \ \ \ \ \ \ \ \ \ \ \ \ \ \ 25x = 750$
    $\ x = \mathbf{30}$

4. $\dfrac{\text{gallons}}{\text{miles}}$ $\quad \dfrac{12}{336}=\dfrac{20}{x}$
$\qquad 12x = 6720$
$\qquad \quad x = \mathbf{560\ mi}$

5. $\dfrac{\text{inches}}{\text{miles}}$ $\quad \dfrac{\frac{1}{4}}{20}=\dfrac{x}{140}$
$\qquad 20x = 35$
$\qquad \quad x = \dfrac{35}{20}=1\dfrac{15}{20}=\mathbf{1\dfrac{3}{4}\ in.}$

6. hamburgers 7
   chicken +3
   total 10

   $\dfrac{\text{chicken}}{\text{total}}$ $\quad \dfrac{3}{10}=\dfrac{x}{430}$
   $\qquad 10x = 1290$
   $\qquad \quad x = \mathbf{129}$

7. made 2
   received +11
   total 13

   $\dfrac{\text{received}}{\text{total}}$ $\quad \dfrac{11}{13}=\dfrac{x}{338}$
   $\qquad 13x = 3718$
   $\qquad \quad x = \mathbf{286}$

8. total 11
   watchers −8
   nonwatchers 3

   $\dfrac{\text{nonwatchers}}{\text{total}}$ $\quad \dfrac{3}{11}=\dfrac{x}{1430}$
   $\qquad 11x = 4290$
   $\qquad \quad x = \mathbf{390}$

9. total 10
   managers −1
   nonmanagers 9

   $\dfrac{\text{nonmanagers}}{\text{total}}$ $\quad \dfrac{9}{10}=\dfrac{648}{x}$
   $\qquad 9x = 6480$
   $\qquad \quad x = \mathbf{720}$

10. adults 9
    children +8
    total 17

    $\dfrac{\text{adults}}{\text{total}}$ $\quad \dfrac{9}{17}=\dfrac{x}{187}$
    $\qquad 17x = 1683$
    $\qquad \quad x = \mathbf{99}$

11. $626 \div \frac{1}{4} = \frac{626}{1} \div \frac{1}{4} = \frac{626}{1} \times \frac{4}{1} = \mathbf{2504}$

12. $\quad 3\frac{1}{8} = 3\frac{2}{16} = 2\frac{2}{16} + \frac{16}{16} \quad = 2\frac{18}{16}$
    $-\ 2\frac{9}{16} = \qquad\qquad\qquad\qquad = 2\frac{9}{16}$
    $\qquad\qquad\qquad\qquad\qquad\qquad\quad \mathbf{\dfrac{9}{16}\ lb}$

13. $10\frac{1}{8} \div 9 = \frac{81}{8} \div \frac{9}{1} = \frac{\cancel{81}^9}{8} \times \frac{1}{\cancel{9}_1} = \mathbf{\dfrac{9}{8}\ ft}$

14. $\dfrac{15 \div 3}{9 \div 3} = \mathbf{\dfrac{5}{3}}$

15. $A = lw$
    $A = 4\frac{1}{2} \times 1\frac{1}{2}$
    $A = \frac{9}{2} \times \frac{3}{2}$
    $A = \frac{27}{4} = \mathbf{6\dfrac{3}{4}\ ft^2}$

16. $\dfrac{4}{6} = \mathbf{\dfrac{2}{3}}$

17. $\frac{1}{8} \times \$1440 = \frac{1}{\cancel{8}} \times \frac{\cancel{\$1440}^{180}}{1} = \mathbf{\$180}$

18. $150 \div 2\frac{1}{2} = \frac{150}{1} \div \frac{5}{2} = \frac{\cancel{150}^{30}}{1} \times \frac{2}{\cancel{5}_1} = \mathbf{60\ mph}$

19. $\frac{5}{6} \times 3252 = \frac{5}{\cancel{6}} \times \frac{\cancel{3252}^{542}}{1} = \mathbf{2710}$

20. $45 \div \frac{3}{4} = \frac{45}{1} \div \frac{3}{4} = \frac{\cancel{45}^{15}}{1} \times \frac{4}{\cancel{3}_1} = \mathbf{60}$

21. (4) $\dfrac{\text{male}}{\text{female}}$ $\quad \dfrac{2}{7}=\dfrac{350}{x}$
    $\qquad 2x = 2450$
    $\qquad \quad x = \mathbf{1225}$

22. (2) $\dfrac{\text{miles}}{\text{hours}}$ $\quad \dfrac{600}{12}=\dfrac{150}{x}$
    $\qquad 600x = 12 \times 150$
    $\qquad \quad x = \mathbf{\dfrac{12 \times 150}{600}}$

23. (4) $\dfrac{\text{inches}}{\text{miles}}$ $\quad \dfrac{\frac{1}{2}}{10}=\dfrac{2\frac{1}{2}}{x}$
    $\qquad \frac{1}{2}x = 10 \times 2\frac{1}{2}$
    $\qquad \frac{1}{2}x = \frac{\cancel{10}^5}{1} \times \frac{5}{\cancel{2}_1}$
    $\qquad \frac{1}{2}x = 25$
    $\qquad \quad x = 25 \div \frac{1}{2}$
    $\qquad \quad x = \frac{25}{1} \times \frac{2}{1}$
    $\qquad \quad x = \mathbf{50\ mi}$

Answer Key, Chapter 3, Level 3   107

24. (3) $\dfrac{\text{muffins}}{\text{cost}} \quad \dfrac{12}{\$7.08} = \dfrac{8}{x}$
$12x = \$56.64$
$x = \mathbf{\$4.72}$

25. (3) $\dfrac{\text{dryers}}{\text{washers}} \quad \dfrac{5}{4} = \dfrac{60}{x}$
$5x = 240$
$x = \mathbf{48}$

26. (2) urban 11
rural + 4
total 15

$\dfrac{\text{rural}}{\text{total}} \quad \dfrac{4}{15} = \dfrac{x}{60{,}000}$
$15x = 240{,}000$
$x = \mathbf{16{,}000}$

27. (5) total 5
night −1
other 4

$\dfrac{\text{other}}{\text{total}} \quad \dfrac{4}{5} = \dfrac{x}{300}$
$5x = 1200$
$x = \mathbf{240}$

28. (5) **Insufficient data is given to solve the problem.** The number of people surveyed or the number of people who said they do not exercise is not given.

29. (3) coats 3
other +5
total 8

$\dfrac{\text{other}}{\text{total}} \quad \dfrac{5}{8} = \dfrac{\$1800}{x}$
$5x = \$14{,}400$
$x = \mathbf{\$2880}$

30. (2) $\dfrac{\text{use}}{\text{do not}} \quad \dfrac{2}{7-2} = \dfrac{x}{64{,}000}$
$(7-2)x = 2 \times 64{,}000$
$x = \dfrac{\mathbf{2 \times 64{,}000}}{\mathbf{7 - 2}}$

31. (2) $204\tfrac{1}{2} = 204\tfrac{2}{4} = 203\tfrac{2}{4} + \tfrac{4}{4} = 203\tfrac{6}{4}$
$-\ 75\tfrac{3}{4} = \qquad\qquad\qquad\quad 75\tfrac{3}{4}$
$\overline{\qquad\qquad\qquad\qquad\qquad\ 128\tfrac{3}{4}\ \mathbf{lb}}$

32. (2) 5 days × 2 trips = 10 trips
$\tfrac{3}{5} \times 10 = \tfrac{3}{\cancel{5}} \times \tfrac{\cancel{10}^{2}}{1} = \mathbf{6\ h}$

33. (3) $4\tfrac{3}{8} \div 7 = \tfrac{35}{8} \div \tfrac{7}{1} = \tfrac{\cancel{35}^{5}}{8} \times \tfrac{1}{\cancel{7}_{1}} = \mathbf{\tfrac{5}{8}\ yd}$

34. (1) $\dfrac{\text{save}}{\text{spend}} \quad \dfrac{2}{5} = \dfrac{x}{\$730}$
$5x = 2 \times \$730$
$x = \dfrac{\mathbf{2 \times \$730}}{\mathbf{5}}$

35. (1) $A = \tfrac{1}{2}bh$
$A = \tfrac{1}{2} \times 4 \times 3$
$A = \tfrac{1}{\cancel{2}} \times \tfrac{\cancel{4}^{2}}{1} \times \tfrac{3}{1}$
$A = \mathbf{6\ ft^2}$

36. (1) $5\tfrac{3}{4} \div 4$
Divide to find each person's share.

37. (2) $207 \div 6\tfrac{9}{10} = \tfrac{207}{1} \div \tfrac{69}{10} =$
$\tfrac{\cancel{207}^{3}}{1} \times \tfrac{10}{\cancel{69}_{1}} = \mathbf{30\ mpg}$

38. (5) **Insufficient data is given to solve the problem.** The number of hours he worked last week is not given.

39. (2) **B, C, A, E, D**
$\tfrac{7 \times 2}{24 \times 2} = \tfrac{14}{48}$
$\tfrac{1 \times 8}{6 \times 8} = \tfrac{8}{48}$
$\tfrac{3 \times 3}{16 \times 3} = \tfrac{9}{48}$
$\tfrac{5 \times 6}{8 \times 6} = \tfrac{30}{48}$
$\tfrac{5 \times 4}{12 \times 4} = \tfrac{20}{48}$

40. (4) $9\tfrac{1}{2} \times 2$
There are 2 pints in every quart.

Chapter 4: Percents

Level 1

1. $0.82 = 0.82\underset{\frown}{} = \mathbf{82\%}$

2. $73\% = \underset{\frown}{}73\% = \mathbf{0.73}$

3. $64\% = \tfrac{64}{100} = \mathbf{\tfrac{16}{25}}$

4. $\tfrac{11}{\cancel{20}} \times \tfrac{\cancel{100}^{5}}{1} = \mathbf{55\%}$

5. $\tfrac{1}{11} \times \tfrac{100}{1} = \tfrac{100}{11} = \mathbf{9\tfrac{1}{11}\%}$

6. $41.5\% = 41\underset{\frown}{}5\% = 0.415$
$\tfrac{415}{1000} = \mathbf{\tfrac{83}{200}}$

7. $0.00125 = 0.00\underset{\frown}{}125 = \mathbf{0.125\%}$

8. $0.072\% = \underset{\frown}{}00.072\% = \mathbf{0.00072}$

9. $5\frac{5}{8}\% = \frac{5\frac{5}{8}}{100}$
   $= 5\frac{5}{8} \div 100 = \frac{45}{8} \div \frac{100}{1}$
   $= \frac{\cancel{45}^9}{8} \times \frac{1}{\cancel{100}_{20}} = \frac{9}{160}$

10. $75\% = \frac{3}{4}$
    $\frac{3}{4} \times 15 = \frac{3}{4} \times \frac{15}{1} = \frac{45}{4} = 11\frac{1}{4}$

11. $0.2\% = 0.002$
    $\quad\quad 0.002$
    $\quad\quad \times \quad 20$
    $\quad\quad 0.040 = \mathbf{0.04}$

12. $\frac{30}{150} = \frac{1}{5}$
    $\frac{1}{\cancel{5}} \times \frac{\cancel{100}^{20}}{1} = \mathbf{20\%}$

13. $\frac{55}{20} = \frac{11}{4}$
    $\frac{11}{\cancel{4}} \times \frac{\cancel{100}^{25}}{1} = \mathbf{275\%}$

14. $\frac{18}{48} = \frac{3}{8}$
    $\frac{3}{\cancel{8}} \times \frac{\cancel{100}^{25}}{1} = \frac{75}{2} = \mathbf{37\frac{1}{2}\%}$

15. $60\% = 0.6$
    $\quad\quad\quad\quad \mathbf{45}$
    $0.6\overline{)27.0\,}$
    $\quad\quad\underline{24}$
    $\quad\quad\;\;3\;0$
    $\quad\quad\;\;\underline{3\;0}$
    $\quad\quad\quad\;\;0$

16. $66\frac{2}{3}\% = \frac{2}{3}$
    $64 \div \frac{2}{3} = \frac{64}{1} \div \frac{2}{3} = \frac{\cancel{64}^{32}}{1} \times \frac{3}{\cancel{2}_1} = \mathbf{96}$

17. $3\% = 0.03$
    $\quad\quad\quad\quad \mathbf{300}$
    $0.03\overline{)9.00\,}$
    $\quad\quad\underline{9}$
    $\quad\quad\,0$

	Fraction	Decimal	Percent
18.	$\frac{1}{3}$	$0.33\frac{1}{3}$	$33\frac{1}{3}\%$
19.	$\frac{5}{6}$	$0.83\frac{1}{3}$	$83\frac{1}{3}\%$
20.	$\frac{1}{8}$	$0.12\frac{1}{2}$	$12\frac{1}{2}\%$

Level 2

1. $50\% = 0.5$
   $\quad\quad\quad \$170$
   $\quad\quad\quad \times \;\; 0.5$
   $\quad\quad\quad \$85.0 = \mathbf{\$85}$

2. $35\% = 0.35 \quad\quad 540$
   $\quad\quad\quad\quad\quad \times\; 0.35$
   $\quad\quad\quad\quad\quad\; 27\,00$
   $\quad\quad\quad\quad\quad\; 162\,0$
   $\quad\quad\quad\quad\quad\overline{189.00} = \mathbf{189}$

3. $12\frac{1}{2}\% = 12.5\% = 0.125 \quad 1398$
   $\quad\quad\quad\quad\quad\quad\quad\quad\quad \times\; 0.125$
   $\quad\quad\quad\quad\quad\quad\quad\quad\quad\; 6990$
   $\quad\quad\quad\quad\quad\quad\quad\quad\quad\; 2796$
   $\quad\quad\quad\quad\quad\quad\quad\quad\quad\; 1398$
   $\quad\quad\quad\quad\quad\quad\quad\quad\overline{174.750} = \mathbf{\$174.75}$

4. $2.5\% = 0.025 \quad 34{,}640$
   $\quad\quad\quad\quad\quad\quad \times\; 0.025$
   $\quad\quad\quad\quad\quad\quad\; 173\,200$
   $\quad\quad\quad\quad\quad\quad\;\;\; 692\,80$
   $\quad\quad\quad\quad\quad\quad\overline{866.000}$
   total $\quad\quad\quad\quad\; 34{,}640$
   didn't like flying - $\;\;\;866$
   liked flying $\quad\quad \overline{33{,}774}$

5. $\frac{\text{won}}{\text{total}} \quad \frac{18}{25}$
   $\frac{18}{\cancel{25}_1} \times \frac{\cancel{100}^4}{1} = \mathbf{72\%}$

6. $\frac{\text{tax}}{\text{cost}} \quad \frac{\$0.75}{\$12.50} = \frac{3}{50}$
   $\frac{3}{\cancel{50}_1} \times \frac{\cancel{100}^2}{1} = \mathbf{6\%}$

7. $\frac{\text{sick}}{\text{total}} \quad \frac{120}{360} = \frac{1}{3} = \mathbf{33\frac{1}{3}\%}$

8. $\frac{\text{deduction}}{\text{earnings}} \quad \frac{\$328}{\$1600} = \frac{41}{200}$
   $\frac{41}{\cancel{200}_2} \times \frac{\cancel{100}^1}{1} = \frac{41}{2} = \mathbf{20\frac{1}{2}\%}$

9. $75\% = 0.75$
   $\quad\quad\quad\quad\quad\quad\; \mathbf{28 \text{ questions}}$
   $\quad\quad\quad\quad 0.75\overline{)21.00\,}$
   $\quad\quad\quad\quad\quad\quad \underline{15\;0}$
   $\quad\quad\quad\quad\quad\quad\;\; 6\;00$
   $\quad\quad\quad\quad\quad\quad\;\; \underline{6\;00}$
   $\quad\quad\quad\quad\quad\quad\quad\quad 0$

10. 20% = 0.2

$$0.2\overline{)\$35.0} = \$175$$

$$\begin{array}{r}2\\\hline 15\\14\\\hline 10\\10\\\hline 0\end{array}$$

11. 27% = 0.27

$$0.27\overline{)\$11{,}070.00} = \$41{,}000$$

$$\begin{array}{r}108\\\hline 27\\27\\\hline 0\end{array}$$

12. $66\frac{2}{3}\% = \frac{2}{3}$

$$114 \div \frac{2}{3} = \frac{\cancel{114}^{57}}{1} \times \frac{3}{\cancel{2}_1} = \mathbf{171}$$

13. $i = prt$

$$i = \frac{\cancel{\$140}^{7}}{1} \times \frac{7}{\cancel{100}_5} \times \frac{3}{1} = \mathbf{\$29.40} \text{ or}$$

$$i = \$140 \times 0.07 \times 3 = \mathbf{\$29.40}$$

14. 6 months = $\frac{1}{2}$ year

$i = prt$

$$i = \frac{\cancel{\$1500}^{15}}{1} \times \frac{\cancel{12}^{6}}{\cancel{100}_1} \times \frac{1}{\cancel{2}_1} = \mathbf{\$90}$$

15. $i = prt$

$$i = \frac{\cancel{\$90}^{9}}{1} \times \frac{4.5}{\cancel{100}_{10}} \times 1 = \mathbf{\$4.05} \text{ or}$$

$$i = \$90 \times 0.045 \times 1 = \mathbf{\$4.05}$$

16. **(3)** 20% = 0.2

$$\begin{array}{r}\$8500\\\times\ \ \ 0.2\\\hline \$1700.0 = \mathbf{\$1700}\end{array}$$

17. **(3)** 5% = 0.05

$$\begin{array}{r}\$11.50\\\times\ \ \ 0.05\\\hline \$0.5750\end{array}$$ rounded to the nearest cent = **$0.58**

18. **(1)** 0.0625 × $7.20

19. **(1)** 35% = 0.35

$$\begin{array}{r}\$55{,}000\\\times\ \ \ \ \ 0.35\\\hline 2750\ 00\\1\ 6500\ 0\\\hline \mathbf{\$19{,}250.00}\end{array}$$

20. **(2)** $\dfrac{\text{hits}}{\text{at bats}}$ $\quad \dfrac{34}{136} = \dfrac{1}{4} = \mathbf{25\%}$

21. **(2)** $\dfrac{\text{defective}}{\text{total}}$ $\quad \dfrac{6}{480} = \dfrac{1}{80} =$

$$\frac{1}{\cancel{80}_4} \times \frac{\cancel{100}^{5}}{1} = \mathbf{1\frac{1}{4}\%}$$

22. **(5) Insufficient data is given to solve the problem.** The total number of words is not given.

23. **(2)** $\dfrac{\text{out}}{\text{total}}$ $\quad \dfrac{5}{21}$

$$\frac{5}{21} \times \frac{100}{1} = \mathbf{\frac{5 \times 100}{21}}$$

24. **(4)** 95% = 0.95

$$0.95\overline{)247.00} = 260$$

$$\begin{array}{r}190\\\hline 57\ 0\\57\ 0\\\hline 0\end{array}$$

25. **(5)** 5% = 0.05

$$0.05\overline{)\$189.23\ 00} = \$37\ 84.60$$

$$\begin{array}{r}15\\\hline 39\\35\\\hline 4\ 2\\4\ 0\\\hline 23\\20\\\hline 3\ 0\\3\ 0\\\hline 0\end{array}$$

26. **(4)** 2.5% = 0.025

$$0.025\overline{)80.000} = 3\ 200$$

$$\begin{array}{r}75\\\hline 5\ 0\\5\ 0\\\hline 0\end{array}$$

27. **(5)** $51 \div 0.34$

28. **(3)** $i = prt$

    $i = \dfrac{{}^{23}\cancel{\$230}}{1} \times \dfrac{6}{\cancel{100}_{{}_{5}}{}^{10}} \times \dfrac{\cancel{2}^{1}}{1} =$

    $\dfrac{\$138}{5} = \$27.60$ or

    $i = \$230 \times 0.06 \times 2 = \$27.60$

29. **(5) Insufficient data is given to solve the problem.** The interest rate is not given.

30. **(4)** $\dfrac{\$172}{1} \times \dfrac{15}{100} \times \dfrac{2}{3}$

    8 months = $\dfrac{2}{3}$ year

Level 3

1. $12\% = 0.12$

    $\$450$
    $\times \;\; 0.12$
    $\overline{9\;00}$
    $\;\;45\;0$
    $\overline{\$\;54.00}$ or

    $\dfrac{p}{\$450} = \dfrac{12}{100}$
    $100p = \$5400$
    $p = \$54$
    $\$450 + \$54 = \mathbf{\$504}$

2. $33\dfrac{1}{3}\% = \dfrac{1}{3}$

    $\dfrac{1}{{}_{1}\cancel{3}} \times \dfrac{\cancel{\$270}^{90}}{1} = \$90$ or

    $\dfrac{p}{\$270} = \dfrac{33\frac{1}{3}}{100}$
    $100p = \$9000$
    $p = \$90$
    $\$270 - \$90 = \mathbf{\$180}$

3. $\$42 + \$28 = \$70;\; 7\% = 0.07$

    $\$70$
    $\times \;\; 0.07$
    $\overline{\$\;\;4.90}$ or

    $\dfrac{p}{\$70} = \dfrac{7}{100}$
    $100p = \$490$
    $p = \$4.90$
    $\$70 + \$4.90 = \mathbf{\$74.90}$

4. **25%** $\$320 - \$240 = \$80$

    $\dfrac{\text{change}}{\text{original}}\quad \dfrac{\$80}{\$320} = \dfrac{1}{4} = 25\%$ or

    $\dfrac{\$80}{\$320} = \dfrac{r}{100}$
    $\$8000 = \$320r$
    $25 = r$

5. **80%** $\$24 + \$96 = \$120$

    $\dfrac{\text{lodging}}{\text{total}}\quad \dfrac{\$96}{\$120} = \dfrac{4}{5}$

    $\dfrac{4}{{}_{1}\cancel{5}} \times \dfrac{\cancel{100}^{20}}{1} = 80\%$ or

    $\dfrac{\$96}{\$120} = \dfrac{r}{100}$
    $\$9600 = \$120r$
    $80 = r$

6. **85%** $\$9900 - \$1485 = \$8415$

    $\dfrac{\text{reduced price}}{\text{sticker price}}\quad \dfrac{\$8415}{\$9900} = \dfrac{153}{180}$

    $\dfrac{153}{{}_{9}\cancel{180}} \times \dfrac{\cancel{100}^{5}}{1} = \dfrac{765}{9} = 85\%$ or

    $\dfrac{\$8415}{\$9900} = \dfrac{r}{100}$
    $\$841{,}500 = \$9900r$
    $\phantom{\$841{,}50}85 = r$

7. **60%** $\$0.48 - \$0.30 = \$0.18$

    $\dfrac{\text{sale price}}{\text{purchase price}}\quad \dfrac{\$0.18}{\$0.30} = \dfrac{3}{5}$

    $\dfrac{3}{{}_{1}\cancel{5}} \times \dfrac{\cancel{100}^{20}}{1} = 60\%$ or

    $\dfrac{\$0.18}{\$0.30} = \dfrac{r}{100}$
    $\$18 = \$0.30r$
    $60 = r$

8. $96\% = 0.96$

$$0.96\overline{)12.00\,0}$$
$$\underline{9\,6}$$
$$2\,40$$
$$\underline{1\,92}$$
$$48\,0$$
$$\underline{48\,0}$$
$$0$$

or

$$\frac{12}{b} = \frac{96}{100}$$
$$1200 = 96b$$
$$12.5 = b$$
$$12.5 - 12 = \textbf{0.5 mi}$$

9. $30\% = 0.3$

$$0.3\overline{)\$456.0}$$
quotient $\$152\,0$
$$\underline{3}$$
$$15$$
$$\underline{15}$$
$$06$$
$$\underline{6}$$
$$0$$

or

$$\frac{\$456}{b} = \frac{30}{100}$$
$$\$45,600 = 30b$$
$$\$1520 = b$$

$\$1520 - \$456 = \textbf{\$1064}$

10. $82\% = 0.82$

$$0.82\overline{)\$6560.00}$$
quotient $\$80\,00$
$$\underline{656}$$
$$0$$

or

$$\frac{\$6560}{b} = \frac{82}{100}$$
$$\$656,000 = 82b$$
$$\$8000 = b$$

$\$8000 - \$6560 = \textbf{\$1440}$

11. $87.5\% = \frac{7}{8}$

$77 \div \frac{7}{8} = \frac{{}^{11}\cancel{77}}{1} \times \frac{8}{\cancel{7}_1} = 88$ or

$$\frac{77}{b} = \frac{87.5}{100}$$
$$7700 = 87.5b$$
$$88 = b$$

total 88
won -77
lost **11 precincts**

12. Kent's raise:
$12.5\% = \frac{1}{8}$

$\frac{1}{\cancel{8}} \times \frac{\cancel{\$9.20}^{1.15}}{1} = \$1.15$ or

$$\frac{p}{\$9.20} = \frac{12.5}{100}$$
$$100p = \$115$$
$$p = \$1.15$$

$\$1.15 - \$0.98 = \textbf{\$0.17}$

13. Leonard's weekly earnings:
$25\% = \frac{1}{4}$

$\frac{1}{4} \times \frac{\$1604}{1} = \$401$ or

$$\frac{p}{\$1604} = \frac{25}{100}$$
$$100p = \$40,100$$
$$p = \$401$$

$\$401 + \$40 = \$441$

Sharon's weekly earnings:
$\$772 \div 2 = \$386$

$\$441 - \$386 = \textbf{\$55}$

14. Groceries:
$30\% = 0.3$

$\$1260$
$\times\ \ 0.3$
$\overline{\$378.0} = \$378$ or

$$\frac{p}{\$1260} = \frac{30}{100}$$
$$100p = \$37,800$$
$$p = \$378$$

$\$415 - \$378 = \textbf{\$37}$

15. First dealer:
 16% = 0.16

$$\begin{array}{r}\$9899\\ \times\ \ \ 0.16\\ \hline 593\ 94\\ 989\ 9\\ \hline \$1583.84\end{array}$$ or

$$\frac{p}{\$9899}=\frac{16}{100}$$
$$100p = \$158,384$$
$$p = \$1583.84$$

$1583.84 - \$1495.00 = $**$88.84**

16. 15% = 0.15

$$\begin{array}{r}\$17,576\\ \times\ \ \ 0.15\\ \hline 878\ 80\\ 1757\ 6\\ \hline \mathbf{\$2636.40}\end{array}$$ or

$$\frac{p}{\$17,576}=\frac{15}{100}$$
$$100p = \$263,640$$
$$p = \mathbf{\$2636.40}$$

17. Income:
 $21,098 + $347 = $21,445

 Net income:
 $21,445 − $5884 = $15,561

 15% = 0.15

$$\begin{array}{r}\$15,561\\ \times\ \ \ 0.15\\ \hline 778\ 05\\ 1556\ 1\\ \hline \mathbf{\$2334.15}\end{array}$$ or

$$\frac{p}{\$15,561}=\frac{15}{100}$$
$$100p = \$233,415$$
$$p = \mathbf{\$2334.15}$$

18. $\dfrac{\text{part}}{\text{total}}\ \ \dfrac{\$512.80}{\$2564}=\dfrac{1}{5}$

$$\frac{1}{\cancel{5}}\times\frac{\cancel{100}^{20}}{1}=\mathbf{20\%}\ \ \text{or}$$

$$\frac{\$512.80}{\$2564}=\frac{r}{100}$$
$$\$51,280 = \$2564r$$
$$r = 20\quad \text{Rate is } \mathbf{20\%}.$$

19. Amount over $27,300:
 $29,000 − $27,300 = $1700

 28% = 0.28

$$\begin{array}{r}\$1700\\ \times\ \ \ 0.28\\ \hline 136\ 00\\ 340\ 0\\ \hline \$476.00\end{array}$$ or

$$\frac{p}{\$1700}=\frac{28}{100}$$
$$100p = \$47,600$$
$$p = \$476$$

 Total tax:
 $4095 + $476 = **$4571**

20. Deductions:
 $3986 + $2539 + $400 = $6925

 Net income:
 $45,765 − $6925 = $38,840

 Amount over $34,000:
 $38,840 − $34,000 = $4840

 28% = 0.28

$$\begin{array}{r}\$4840\\ \times\ \ \ 0.28\\ \hline 387\ 20\\ 968\ 0\\ \hline \$1355.20\end{array}$$ or

$$\frac{p}{\$4840}=\frac{28}{100}$$
$$100p = \$135,520$$
$$p = \$1355.20$$

 Total tax:
 $5100 + $1355.20 = **$6455.20**

Answer Key, Chapter 4, Level 3   113

21. (2) $32\% = 0.32$

$$\begin{array}{r} 175 \\ \times\ 0.32 \\ \hline 3\,50 \\ 52\,5 \\ \hline 56.00 \end{array}$$ or

$$\frac{p}{175} = \frac{32}{100}$$
$$100p = 5600$$
$$p = 56$$

$175 - 56 = \textbf{119 lb}$

22. (4) $40\% = 0.4$

$$\begin{array}{r} \$1.20 \\ \times\ \ 0.4 \\ \hline \$0.480 = \$0.48 \end{array}$$ or

$$\frac{p}{\$1.20} = \frac{40}{100}$$
$$100p = \$48$$
$$p = \$0.48$$

$\$1.20 + \$0.48 = \textbf{\$1.68}$

23. (5) $\$420 - (\frac{1}{4} \times \$420)$

Subtract the down payment, 25% or $\frac{1}{4}$ of $420, from the price.

24. (3) $90\% = 0.9$

$$\begin{array}{r} \$40 \\ \times\ \ 0.9 \\ \hline \$36.0 = \$36 \end{array}$$ or

$$\frac{p}{\$40} = \frac{90}{100}$$
$$100p = \$3600$$
$$p = \$36$$

$\$40 + \$36 = \textbf{\$76}$

25. (1) $\$9500 - \$5700 = \$3800$

$$\frac{\text{change}}{\text{original}} = \frac{\$3800}{\$9500} = \frac{2}{5}$$

$$\frac{2}{\cancel{5}} \times \frac{\cancel{100}^{20}}{1} = \textbf{40\%}$$ or

$$\frac{\$3800}{\$9500} = \frac{r}{100}$$
$$\$380,000 = \$9500r$$
$$r = 40 \quad \text{Rate is } \textbf{40\%}.$$

26. (4) $\dfrac{\$86 - \$73.10}{\$86} \times 100$

27. (5) Insufficient data is given to solve the problem. The population in 1980 is not given.

28. (2) $37.5\% = \dfrac{3}{8}$

$$45 \div \frac{3}{8} = \frac{45}{1} \div \frac{3}{8} = \frac{\cancel{45}^{15}}{1} \times \frac{8}{\cancel{3}_1} = 120$$ or

$$\frac{45}{b} = \frac{37.5}{100}$$
$$4500 = 37.5b$$
$$120 = b$$

$120 - 45 = \textbf{75}$

29. (2) $80\% = 0.8$

$$\begin{array}{r} \$206.25 \\ 0.8)\overline{\$165.0\,00} \\ \underline{16} \\ 5\,0 \\ \underline{4\,8} \\ 20 \\ \underline{16} \\ 40 \\ \underline{40} \\ 0 \end{array}$$ or

$$\frac{\$165}{b} = \frac{80}{100}$$
$$\$16,500 = 80b$$
$$\$206.25 = b$$

$\$206.25 - \$165 = \textbf{\$41.25}$

30. **(3)** 5% = 0.05

$$0.05\overline{)2.00}$$ or
 $$\underline{2\,0}$$
 $$0$$

$$\frac{2}{b} = \frac{5}{100}$$
$$200 = 5b$$
$$40 = b$$

$$40 + 2 = \mathbf{42}$$

31. **(5)** $\dfrac{\$294{,}912}{0.72} - \$294{,}912$

Subtract expenses from gross sales.

32. **(3) 7% on a purchase of $0.95**

(1) $0.05 \times \$1.00 = \$0.05$ or

$$\frac{p}{\$1.00} = \frac{5}{100}$$
$$100p = \$5.00$$
$$p = \$0.05$$

(2) $0.03 \times \$1.75 = \$0.0525$ or

$$\frac{p}{\$1.75} = \frac{3}{100}$$
$$100p = \$5.25$$
$$p = \$0.0525$$

(3) $0.07 \times \$0.95 = \$0.0665$ or

$$\frac{p}{\$0.95} = \frac{7}{100}$$
$$100p = \$6.65$$
$$p = \$0.0665$$

(4) $0.04 \times \$1.50 = \$0.06$ or

$$\frac{p}{\$1.50} = \frac{4}{100}$$
$$100p = \$6.00$$
$$p = \$0.06$$

(5) $0.02 \times \$2.50 = \$0.05$ or

$$\frac{p}{\$2.50} = \frac{2}{100}$$
$$100p = \$5.00$$
$$p = \$0.05$$

33. **(4) Taking a job that pays $420 per week**

(1) $0.2 \times \$15{,}000 = \$3000$ or

$$\frac{p}{\$15{,}000} = \frac{20}{100}$$
$$100p = \$300{,}000$$
$$p = \$3000$$

$$\$15{,}000 + \$3000 = \$18{,}000$$

(2) $12 \times \$1250 = \$15{,}000$

(3) $0.03 \times \$150{,}000 = \$4500$ or

$$\frac{p}{\$150{,}000} = \frac{3}{100}$$
$$100p = \$450{,}000$$
$$p = \$4500$$

(4) $52 \times \$420 = \$21{,}840$

(5) $18{,}600$

34. **(5) Insurance payments as follows: medical, $750; auto, $598; and life, $621**

(1) $984

(2) $0.04 \times \$29{,}500 = \$1180$ or

$$\frac{p}{\$29{,}500} = \frac{4}{100}$$
$$100p = \$118{,}000$$
$$p = \$1180$$

(3) $12 \times \$129 = \$1548$

(4) $0.12 \times \$10{,}800 = \$1296$ or

$$\frac{p}{\$10{,}800} = \frac{12}{100}$$
$$100p = \$129{,}600$$
$$p = \$1296$$

(5) $\$750 + \$598 + \$621 = \$1969$

35. **(1) Frank gets an 8% commission on sales of $4000 plus a salary of $150.**

(1) $0.08 \times \$4000 = \$320$ or

$$\frac{p}{\$4000} = \frac{8}{100}$$
$$100p = \$32{,}000$$
$$p = \$320$$

$\$320 + \$150 = \$470$

(2) $0.1 \times \$4900 = \$490$ or

$$\frac{p}{\$4900} = \frac{10}{100}$$
$$100p = \$49{,}000$$
$$p = \$490$$

(3) $0.2 \times \$2000 = \$400$ or

$$\frac{p}{\$2000} = \frac{20}{100}$$
$$100p = \$40{,}000$$
$$p = \$400$$

$0.25 \times \$300 = \$75$ or

$$\frac{p}{\$300} = \frac{25}{100}$$
$$100p = \$7500$$
$$p = \$75$$

$\$400 + \$75 = \$475$

(4) $0.2 \times \$3000 = \$600$ or

$$\frac{p}{\$3000} = \frac{20}{100}$$
$$100p = \$60{,}000$$
$$p = \$600$$

(5) $0.4 \times \$1400 = \$560$ or

$$\frac{p}{\$1400} = \frac{40}{100}$$
$$100p = \$56{,}000$$
$$p = \$560$$

36. (1) $38\% = 0.38$

$$\begin{array}{r} 9800 \\ \times\ \ 0.38 \\ \hline 784\ 00 \\ 2940\ 0 \\ \hline 3724.00 \end{array}$$ or

$$\frac{p}{9800} = \frac{38}{100}$$
$$100p = 372{,}400$$
$$p = 3724$$

$9800 + 3724 = \mathbf{13{,}524}$

37. (3) $2\% = 0.02$

$$\begin{array}{r} 6{,}326{,}000 \\ \times\ \ \ \ \ 0.02 \\ \hline \mathbf{126{,}520}.00 \end{array}$$ or

$$\frac{p}{6{,}326{,}000} = \frac{2}{100}$$
$$100p = 12{,}652{,}000$$
$$p = \mathbf{126{,}520}$$

38. (5) $5\% = 0.05$

$$0.05 \overline{)374.00} = 7480 \text{ or}$$

$$\frac{374}{b} = \frac{5}{100}$$
$$37{,}400 = 5b$$
$$7480 = b$$

$$7480 + 374 = \mathbf{7854}$$

39. (2) $\dfrac{\text{change}}{\text{original}}$ $\dfrac{5000}{40{,}000} = \dfrac{1}{8} = \mathbf{12\dfrac{1}{2}\%}$ or

$$\frac{5000}{40{,}000} = \frac{r}{100}$$
$$500{,}000 = 40{,}000r$$
$$r = 12\frac{1}{2}$$

Rate is $12\dfrac{1}{2}\%$.

40. (4) Albatron:
$6\% = 0.06$

$$\begin{array}{r}356{,}000 \\ \times 0.06 \\ \hline 21{,}360.00 \end{array}$$ or

$$\frac{p}{356{,}000} = \frac{6}{100}$$
$$100p = 2{,}136{,}000$$
$$p = 21{,}360$$

$356{,}000 + 21{,}360 = 377{,}360$

Cattleville:
$350{,}000 + 78{,}000 = 428{,}000$
$428{,}000 - 377{,}360 = \mathbf{50{,}640}$

Chapter 5: Graphs

1. $2 \times 10{,}000 = \mathbf{20{,}000}$ **metric tons**

2. **United States**

3. $\dfrac{2.5}{0.5} = \mathbf{5}$

4. $6 - 4 = 2$
   $2 \times 10{,}000 = \mathbf{20{,}000}$ **metric tons**

5. $0.2 \times 6 = 1.2$ or
   $$\frac{p}{6} = \frac{20}{100}$$
   $$100p = 120$$
   $$p = 1.2$$
   $1.2 \times 10{,}000 = \mathbf{12{,}000}$ **metric tons**

6. $1.5 \times \$129 = \$193.5$
   $\$193.5 \times 10{,}000 = \mathbf{\$1{,}935{,}000}$

7. $\dfrac{490{,}000}{10{,}000} = \mathbf{49}$

8. $5¢ = \dfrac{5}{100} = \mathbf{5\%}$

9. **Promotional**

10. $\dfrac{\text{disaster relief}}{\text{total}}$ $\dfrac{12}{100} = \dfrac{\mathbf{3}}{\mathbf{25}}$

11. **Disaster relief and administrative**
    $12¢ + 9¢ = 21¢$
    $$\frac{1}{\,_1\cancel{5}} \times \frac{\cancel{100}¢^{20}}{1} = 20¢$$

12. $\dfrac{\text{humanitarian service}}{\text{total}}$ $\dfrac{\$0.65}{\$1} = \dfrac{x}{\$2 \text{ million}}$
    $\mathbf{\$1.3 \text{ million}} = x$

13. $6¢ - 5¢ = 1¢$
    $\dfrac{\text{vocational training vs. emergency}}{\text{total}}$ $\dfrac{\$0.01}{\$1} = \dfrac{x}{\$2 \text{ million}}$
    $\$0.02 \text{ million} = x$
    $\$0.02 \text{ million} = \mathbf{\$20{,}000}$

14. **Mining**

15. **Services**

16. Transportation/Utilities

17. Retail trade: approximately $175
    Manufacturing: approximately $425

    $425 − $175 = **$250**

18. Transportation/utilities weekly earnings: approximately $475

    52 × $475 = **$24,700** or

    $$\frac{\text{weekly}}{\text{annual}} \quad \frac{\$475}{x} = \frac{1}{52}$$
    $$\$24,700 = x$$

19. Mining weekly earnings: approximately $550

    $550 ÷ 40 = **$13.75** or

    $$\frac{\text{hourly}}{\text{weekly}} \quad \frac{x}{\$550} = \frac{1}{40}$$
    $$40x = \$550$$
    $$x = \$13.75$$

20. **Alaska, Vermont, Washington**

21. **Wisconsin**

22. Idaho's highest point: approximately 12,000 ft
    Idaho's lowest point: approximately 1000 ft

    12,000 − 1000 = **11,000 ft**

23. Wyoming's highest point: approximately 14,000 ft
    Minnesota's highest point: approximately 2000 ft

    $$\frac{14{,}000}{2{,}000} = \mathbf{7}$$

24. **1950**

25. **1970**

26. **1964**

27. **15,000**

28. **20,000**

29. Branches in 1980: approximately 40,000
    Banks in 1980: approximately 15,000
    40,000 − 15,000 = **25,000**

30. The steepest part of the line for branches is from **1970 to 1980**.

31. (4) **San Diego Padres**

32. (4) $2(11 + 5\frac{1}{2})$
    Multiply the total number of symbols by the number each symbol represents.

33. (1) $\dfrac{\text{wins}}{\text{totals}}$ $\dfrac{1}{\cancel{5}} \times \dfrac{\cancel{100}^{20}}{1} = \mathbf{20\%}$ or

    $$\frac{1}{5} = \frac{r}{100}$$
    $$100 = 5r$$
    $$20 = r \quad \text{Rate is } \mathbf{20\%}.$$

34. (3) Red Sox: $2(2\frac{1}{2} + 2) = 9$
    Orioles: $2(1\frac{1}{2} + 1\frac{1}{2}) = 6$
    $9 - 6 = \mathbf{3}$

35. (5) **Insufficient data is given to solve the problem.** The number of games played in each World Series is not given.

36. (3) Wins: $\dfrac{1}{2} \times 2 = 1$

    Total World Series played:
    $$2\left(\frac{1}{2} + 1\frac{1}{2}\right) = 4$$

    $$\frac{\text{wins}}{\text{total}} \quad \frac{1}{4} = \frac{6}{x}$$
    $$x = \mathbf{24}$$

37. (4) $100\% - 32\% = 68\% = \dfrac{68}{100} = \dfrac{\mathbf{17}}{\mathbf{25}}$

38. (1) **Speeding**
    $$\frac{1}{\cancel{5}} \times \frac{\cancel{100}^{20}}{1} = 20\%$$

39. **(3)** Total accidents:
32% = 0.32

$$0.32 \overline{\smash{)}4.20\,000} = 13.125 \text{ million or million}$$
$$\underline{3\,2}$$
$$1\,00$$
$$\underline{96}$$
$$4\,0$$
$$\underline{3\,2}$$
$$80$$
$$\underline{64}$$
$$160$$
$$\underline{160}$$
$$0$$

$$\frac{4.2 \text{ million}}{b} = \frac{32}{100}$$
420 million = 32b
13.125 million = b
13.125 million − 4.2 million =
8.925 million

40. **(2)** $\frac{1}{5} \times \frac{13}{1}$

Multiply $\frac{1}{5}$ times the percent of total accidents due to other improper driving, 13%.

41. **(5)** 100% − 39.4% = **60.6%**

42. **(2)** 6.4% is approximately 6%.
$$\frac{15-24}{45-64} \quad \frac{6\%}{24\%} = \frac{1}{4}$$

43. **(5) Insufficient data is given to solve the problem.** The total number of people living alone is not given.

44. **(4)** Of the choices given, the one with the longest bar is **a 7-year-old in a family with girls only.**

45. **(5)** 7-year-old: approximately $2.50
10-year old: approximately $4.30
$4.30 − $2.50 = **$1.80**

46. **(5) Insufficient data is given to solve the problem.** Whether the 5-year-old has any brothers is not given.

47. **(2) A 7-year-old in a family with boys only**

48. **(4)** 52($2.40 + $3.10 + $4.20). Use the bars for boys and girls. Add the average weekly allowances and multiply by the number of weeks in a year.

49. **(1)** 4 − 3 = **1**

50. **(2)** $\frac{\text{federal government}}{\text{total government}} \quad \frac{1}{5} \times \frac{100}{1} = \frac{100}{5}\%$
= **20%** or
$$\frac{1}{5} = \frac{r}{100}$$
100 = 5r
20 = r   Rate is **20%**.

51. **(1)** $\frac{9.0}{18.5}$ is approximately $\frac{9}{18}$, or $\frac{1}{2}$.

52. **(1) The number of employees in local government increased at a greater rate than the number in other levels of government.**

53. **(1) 1984**

54. **(4) 1986 and 1987**

55. **(2)** Approximately 550,000 + 600,000 = 1,150,000, which is **less than 1,200,000.**

56. **(4)** $\frac{100(6.5-5.5)}{5.5}$
$\frac{\text{change}}{1983} \quad \frac{6.5-5.5}{5.5} \times \frac{100}{1}$

57. **(2) 1977**

58. **(1) 2 thousand less**
U.S.: approximately 11 thousand
Japan: approximately 13 thousand
13 thousand − 11 thousand = 2 thousand

59. **(5) Insufficient data is given to solve the problem.** The number of motor vehicles produced in other countries or the total number of motor vehicles produced throughout the world is not given.

60. **(2)** $\frac{5}{8+5}$

Chapter 6: Algebra

Level 1

1. A
2. $-9\dfrac{1}{2}$
3. $-5 + (+4) + (-8) =$
   $-13 + 4 = \textbf{-9}$
4. $(-8) + (+15) + (-16) + (+9) =$
   $-24 + 24 = \textbf{0}$
5. $(+9) - (-6) =$
   $+9 + 6 = \textbf{15}$
6. $(+2) - (-1) + (-10) =$
   $+3 + (-10) = \textbf{-7}$
7. $(6)(-3)\left(-\dfrac{1}{2}\right) = \textbf{9}$
8. $(-8)(2)(-5)(-4) = \textbf{-320}$
9. $\dfrac{-28}{-7} = \textbf{4}$
10. $\dfrac{240}{-60} = \textbf{-4}$
11. $5t + 9t = \textbf{14t}$
12. $d + (-8d) + 34d =$
    $35d + (-8d) = \textbf{27d}$
13. $(5ry) - (-12ry) =$
    $5ry + 12ry = \textbf{17ry}$
14. $(7gk) + (-25gk) - (4gk) =$
    $7gk + (-25gk) + (-4gk) =$
    $7gk + (-29gk) = \textbf{-22gk}$
15. $q \cdot q^3 = \textbf{q}^\textbf{4}$
16. $(-5d^4f^2)(4d^9f^4) = -20d^{13}f^{6}$
17. $\dfrac{-18c^4d^2}{6c^6d^2} = \dfrac{\textbf{-3}}{\textbf{c}^\textbf{2}}$
18. $y - w = (-12) - (-20) =$
    $-12 + 20 = \textbf{8}$
19. $q(q + h) = 9[9 + (-5)] = 9(4) = \textbf{36}$
20. $(b - a)^2 = [-5 - (-8)]^2 = (-5 + 8)^2 = 3^2 = \textbf{9}$

Level 2

1. $\dfrac{9x}{9} = \dfrac{99}{9}$
   $x = \textbf{11}$

2. $\begin{array}{rl} 165 = & w - 87 \\ +87 & +87 \\ \hline \textbf{252} = & w \end{array}$

3. $\begin{array}{rl} 4x - 7 = & 33 \\ +7 & +7 \\ \hline \dfrac{4x}{4} = & \dfrac{40}{4} \\ x = & \textbf{10} \end{array}$

4. $\begin{array}{rl} -2 = & \dfrac{n}{3} + 1 \\ -1 & -1 \\ \hline 3 \cdot (-3) = & \dfrac{n}{3} \cdot 3 \\ \textbf{-9} = & n \end{array}$

5. $a - 5a = 24$
   $\dfrac{-4a}{-4} = \dfrac{24}{-4}$
   $a = \textbf{-6}$

6. $\begin{array}{rl} k - 28 = & 4 - 3k \\ +3k & +3k \\ \hline 4k - 28 = & 4 \\ +28 & +28 \\ \hline \dfrac{4k}{4} = & \dfrac{32}{4} \\ k = & \textbf{8} \end{array}$

7. $8z - 15 = 5(6 + z)$
   $\begin{array}{rl} 8z - 15 = & 30 + 5z \\ -5z & -5z \\ \hline 3z - 15 = & 30 \\ +15 & +15 \\ \hline \dfrac{3z}{3} = & \dfrac{45}{3} \\ z = & \textbf{15} \end{array}$

8. $\begin{array}{rl} x - 9 > & 47 \\ +9 & +9 \\ \hline x > & \textbf{56} \end{array}$

9. $\begin{array}{rl} 7c + 92 \leq & 141 \\ -92 & -92 \\ \hline \dfrac{7c}{7} \leq & \dfrac{49}{7} \\ c \leq & \textbf{7} \end{array}$

120 Answer Key, Chapter 6, Levels 1-2

10.
$$\begin{array}{r} y+4 \\ \times \quad y+6 \\ \hline 6y+24 \\ y^2+4y \quad\quad \\ \hline \mathbf{y^2+10y+24} \end{array}$$

11.
$$\begin{array}{r} x-3 \\ \times \quad x+2 \\ \hline 2x-6 \\ x^2-3x \quad\quad \\ \hline \mathbf{x^2-\ x-6} \end{array}$$

12. **4(5x + 4)**

13. **(x + 2)(x − 9)**. The only factors of -18 that could give the middle term -7x are 2 and -9.

14. $t^2 + 3t - 28 = 0$
$(t+7)(t-4) = 0$
$t+7 = 0$ or $t-4 = 0$
$\dfrac{-7\ \ -7}{t\ \ =-7}$ $\dfrac{+4\ \ +4}{t\ \ =\ 4}$

15. $s^2 - 36 = 0$
$(s+6)(s-6) = 0$
$s+6 = 0$ or $s-6 = 0$
$\dfrac{-6\ \ -6}{s\ \ =-6}$ $\dfrac{+6\ \ +6}{s\ \ =\ 6}$

16. $\sqrt{48} = \sqrt{16} \cdot \sqrt{3} = 4\sqrt{3}$

17. **(3)** $\tfrac{6}{5} \cdot \tfrac{5}{6} h = 35 \cdot \tfrac{6}{5}$
         $h = \mathbf{42}$

18. **(1)** $3 - 5m = 28$
$\dfrac{-3 \qquad\qquad -3}{\ }$
$\dfrac{-5m}{-5} = \dfrac{25}{-5}$
$m = \mathbf{-5}$

19. **(4)** $81 = \tfrac{2}{3}k + 9$
$\dfrac{-9 \qquad\qquad -9}{\ }$
$\tfrac{3}{2} \cdot 72 = \tfrac{2}{3}k \cdot \tfrac{3}{2}$
$\mathbf{108} = k$

20. **(4)** $5x + 3 = 11x - 27$
$\dfrac{-5x \qquad\quad -5x}{\ }$
$3 = 6x - 27$
$\dfrac{+27 \qquad\quad +27}{\ }$
$\dfrac{30}{6} = \dfrac{6x}{6}$
$\mathbf{5} = x$

21. **(3)** $3(r-3) = 27$
$3r - 9 = 27$
$\dfrac{+9 \quad\ +9}{\ }$
$\dfrac{3r}{3} = \dfrac{36}{3}$
$r = \mathbf{12}$

22. **(3)** $d + 6 = 5(d-2)$
$d + 6 = 5d - 10$
$\dfrac{+10 \qquad\quad +10}{\ }$
$d + 16 = 5d$
$\dfrac{-d \qquad\quad -d}{\ }$
$\dfrac{16}{4} = \dfrac{4d}{4}$
$\mathbf{4} = d$

23. **(1)** $7y + 1 \le 6y - 5$
$\dfrac{-6y \qquad\quad -6y}{\ }$
$y + 1 \le -5$
$\dfrac{-1 \qquad\qquad -1}{\ }$
$y \le -6$

24. **(1)** $5(q-3) < 10$
$5q - 15 < 10$
$\dfrac{+15 \qquad +15}{\ }$
$\dfrac{5q}{5} < \dfrac{25}{5}$
$q < 5$
3 is less than 5.

25. **(4)**
$$\begin{array}{r} p-3 \\ \times \quad p-3 \\ \hline -3p+9 \\ p^2-3p \quad\quad \\ \hline \mathbf{p^2-6p+9} \end{array}$$

26. **(3)** $m(m - 2)$

27. **(3)** $(h + 4)(h - 12)$ The only factors of 48 that could give the middle term -8h are 4 and -12.

28. **(4)** $w^2 + 25w + 100 = 0$
$(w+5)(w+20) = 0$
$w+5 = 0$ or $w+20 = 0$
$\dfrac{-5\ \ -5}{w\ \ =-5}$ $\dfrac{-20\ \ -20}{w\ \ =-20}$

Answer Key, Chapter 6, Level 2

29. (3) $b^2 - 2b - 15 = 0$
$(b+3)(b-5) = 0$

$$\begin{array}{rl} b+3 = 0 & b-5 = 0 \\ \underline{-3} \quad \underline{-3} & \underline{+5} \quad \underline{+5} \\ b = -3 & b = 5 \end{array}$$ or

30. (4) $\sqrt{162} = \sqrt{81} \cdot \sqrt{2} = \mathbf{9\sqrt{2}}$

Level 3

1. $\mathbf{28 + x}$

2. $\mathbf{9(x - 7)}$

3. $\mathbf{\frac{5}{8}x + 21}$

4. $\mathbf{40h}$

5. $\mathbf{t + 8}$

6. $\mathbf{\dfrac{350}{x}}$

7. $3 - 2x = 15$
$\underline{-3} \qquad \underline{-3}$
$\dfrac{-2x}{-2} = \dfrac{12}{-2}$
$x = \mathbf{-6}$

8. $\frac{1}{2}x + 7 = 22$
$\underline{\quad -7} \quad \underline{-7}$
$2 \cdot \frac{1}{2}x = 15 \cdot 2$
$x = \mathbf{30}$

9. $x + 5 = 2x - 3$
$\underline{+3} \quad \underline{+3}$
$x + 8 = 2x$
$\underline{-x} \quad \underline{-x}$
$\mathbf{8} = x$

10. $5(x+5) = 40$
$5x + 25 = 40$
$\underline{\quad -25} \quad \underline{-25}$
$\dfrac{5x}{5} = \dfrac{15}{5}$
$x = \mathbf{3}$

11. $c = nr$
$\$5.61 = 3r$
$\dfrac{\$5.61}{3} = \dfrac{3r}{3}$
$\mathbf{\$1.87} = r$

12. $V = lwh$
$200 = 5 \times w \times 10$
$\dfrac{200}{50} = \dfrac{50w}{50}$
$\mathbf{4} = w$

13. $i = prt$
$\$6.84 = p \times 0.06 \times 3$
$\dfrac{\$6.84}{0.18} = \dfrac{0.18p}{0.18}$
$\mathbf{\$38} = p$

14. $d = rt$
$162 = r \cdot 3$
$\dfrac{162}{3} = \dfrac{3r}{3}$
$\mathbf{54} = r$

15. $A = s^2$
$169 = s^2$
$\sqrt{169} = \sqrt{s^2}$
$\mathbf{13} = s$

16. small number $= x$
large number $= 3x$
$3x - 11 = x - 1$
$\underline{-x} \qquad \underline{-x}$
$2x - 11 = -1$
$\underline{+11} \quad \underline{+11}$
$\dfrac{2x}{2} = \dfrac{10}{2}$
$x = \mathbf{5}$
$3x = 3(5) = \mathbf{15}$

17. education $= e$
highways $= 2e$
$e + 2e = \$12$ million
$\dfrac{3e}{3} = \dfrac{\$12 \text{ million}}{3}$
$e = \mathbf{\$4 \text{ million}}$

18. adult's jacket $= j$
child's jacket $= j - 3$
$j + j - 3 = 11$
$2j - 3 = 11$
$\underline{\quad +3} \quad \underline{+3}$
$\dfrac{2j}{2} = \dfrac{14}{2}$
$j = 7$
$j - 3 = 7 - 3 = \mathbf{4}$

122   Answer Key, Chapter 6, Levels 2-3

19. people at Heather's office = x
    people at Joey's office = $2x + 10$

$$\begin{aligned} x + 2x + 10 &= 73 \\ 3x + 10 &= 73 \\ -10 & -10 \\ \hline \frac{3x}{3} &= \frac{63}{3} \\ x &= 21 \end{aligned}$$

$2x + 10 = 2(21) + 10 = \mathbf{52}$

20.
	Age now	Age in 5 years
Aaron	x	$x + 5$
Mark	$4x$	$4x + 5$

$$\begin{aligned} 4x + 5 &= 3(x + 5) - 1 \\ 4x + 5 &= 3x + 15 - 1 \\ 4x + 5 &= 3x + 14 \\ -3x & -3x \\ \hline x + 5 &= 14 \\ -5 & -5 \\ \hline x &= 9 \end{aligned}$$

$4x = 4(9) = \mathbf{36}$

21. (4) $12x$

22. (3) $\frac{1}{2}x(x - 3)$

23. (4) $\frac{x - 4}{6}$

24. (2) $\frac{1}{4}m$

25. (4) $e - 5$

26. (3) $\frac{\$4.12}{p}$

27. (4) $\frac{x}{3} - 2 = 10$

28. (2)
$$\begin{aligned} 32 - 3x &= 5 \\ -32 & -32 \\ \hline \frac{-3x}{-3} &= \frac{-27}{-3} \\ x &= 9 \end{aligned}$$

29. (2)
$$\frac{(x + 15)}{8} = 4$$
$$8 \cdot \frac{(x + 15)}{8} = 4 \cdot 8$$
$$\begin{aligned} x + 15 &= 32 \\ -15 & -15 \\ \hline x &= \mathbf{17} \end{aligned}$$

30. (5)
$$\begin{aligned} \tfrac{1}{4}x + 9 &= x - 39 \\ +39 & +39 \\ \hline \tfrac{1}{4}x + 48 &= x \\ -\tfrac{1}{4}x & -\tfrac{1}{4}x \\ \hline \tfrac{4}{3} \cdot 48 &= \tfrac{3}{4}x \cdot \tfrac{4}{3} \\ \mathbf{64} &= x \end{aligned}$$

31. (3) 9%
$$i = prt$$
$$\$27 = \$300 \cdot r \cdot 1$$
$$\frac{\$27}{\$300} = \frac{\$300r}{\$300}$$
$$0.09 = r$$

32. (3)
$$c = nr$$
$$\frac{\$1.56}{12} = \frac{12r}{12}$$
$$\mathbf{\$0.13} = r$$

33. (4)
$$d = rt$$
$$\frac{3416}{488} = \frac{488t}{488}$$
$$7 = t$$

34. (5) **Insufficient data is given to solve the problem.** The interest rate is not given.

35. (2)
$$A = \frac{1}{2}bh$$
$$\frac{150}{25} = \frac{\frac{1}{2} \cdot b \cdot 25}{25}$$
$$2 \cdot 6 = \frac{1}{2} \cdot b \cdot 2$$
$$\mathbf{12} = b$$

36. (4) small number = x
    large number = $5x$
    $x + 41 = 9 \times 5x$

Answer Key, Chapter 6, Level 3

37. **(1)** Ernest's fish = x
    Lois's fish = $x - 5$
    $x + x - 5 = 33$
    $2x - 5 = 33$
    $ +5 +5$
    $\dfrac{2x}{2} = \dfrac{38}{2}$
    $x = 19$
    $x - 5 = 19 - 5 = \mathbf{14}$

38. **(2)** bags Chris sold = p
    bags Norm sold = $p + 4$
    bags Bill sold = $5(p + 4)$

    $p + p + 4 + 5(p + 4) = 115$
    $p + p + 4 + 5p + 20 = 115$
    $7p + 24 = 115$
    $ -24 -24$
    $\dfrac{7p}{7} = \dfrac{91}{7}$
    $p = 13$

    $p + 4 = 13 + 4 = \mathbf{17}$

39. **(3)** 4% = 0.04
    cost of car = x
    sales tax = $0.04x$
    $x + 0.04x = \$10{,}250.24$

40. **(5) Insufficient data is given to solve the problem.** The price for which the Ferbers sold their house is not given.

Chapter 7: Geometry

Level 1

1. **Obtuse**

2. **Straight**

3. $180° - 32° = \mathbf{148°}$

4. **Acute**

5. $90° - 12° = \mathbf{78°}$

6. **47°.** Angles s and u are vertical angles.

7. **Angle r**

8. **Reflex**

9. **Angle b**

10. **They are alternate interior angles.**

11. **Angle d**

12. **They are supplementary.**

13. **66°.** Angles n and q are vertical angles.

14. $180° - 66° = \mathbf{114°}$. Angles m and q are supplementary angles.

15. **66°.** Angles k and q are corresponding angles.

16. **66°.** Angles p and q are alternate exterior angles.

17. Triangle ABC is an isosceles triangle.
    $79° + 79° = 158°$
    $180° - 158° = \mathbf{22°}$

18. $90° + 27° = 117°$
    $180° - 117° = \mathbf{63°}$

19. **TW**
    Find the measure of angle W.
    $50° + 97° = 147°$
    $180° - 147° = 33°$
    Since angle P is the largest angle, the side opposite it is the longest side.

20. **Equilateral.** Notice the two equal sides and the vertex measuring 60°.

Level 2

1. $65° + 55° = 120°$
   $180° - 120° = \mathbf{60°}$

2. $\dfrac{GI}{GH} = \dfrac{LN}{LM}$
   $\dfrac{7}{8} = \dfrac{x}{24}$
   $\dfrac{8x}{8} = \dfrac{168}{8}$
   $x = \mathbf{21 \text{ in.}}$

3. **SAS** (side, angle, side)

4. **Corresponding angles are not equal.**

5. **All corresponding sides are not equal.**

6. $12^2 + 16^2 = 144 + 256 = 400$
   $\sqrt{400} = \mathbf{20 \text{ in.}}$

7. $AC^2 + 12^2 = 13^2$
   $AC^2 + 144 = 169$
   $AC^2 = 169 - 144$
   $AC^2 = 25$
   $AC = \textbf{5 in.}$

8. $x^2 + 15^2 = 17^2$
   $x^2 + 225 = 289$
   $x^2 = 289 - 225$
   $x^2 = 64$
   $x = \textbf{8 in.}$

9. **(-5, 3)**

10. **D**

11. $H = (2, 7)$
    $G = (10, 1)$
    $d = \sqrt{(10-2)^2 + (1-7)^2}$
    $= \sqrt{(8)^2 + (-6)^2}$
    $= \sqrt{64 + 36}$
    $= \sqrt{100}$
    $= \textbf{10}$

12. $D = (1, -7)$
    $E = (7, -1)$
    $M = \left(\dfrac{1+7}{2}, \dfrac{(-7)+(-1)}{2}\right)$
    $= \left(\dfrac{8}{2}, \dfrac{-8}{2}\right)$
    $= \textbf{(4, -4)}$

13. $I = (8, 4)$
    $J = (-6, -3)$
    $m = \dfrac{-3-4}{-6-8}$
    $= \dfrac{-7}{-14}$
    $= \dfrac{\textbf{1}}{\textbf{2}}$

14. **(-13, -4)**
    $x = 3(-4) - 1$
    $x = -12 - 1$
    $x = -13$

15. **(9, 96)**
    $y = 9^2 + 2(9) - 3$
    $y = 81 + 18 - 3$
    $y = 96$

16. (5) $\dfrac{120}{10+6}$
    $\dfrac{BR}{TB} = \dfrac{ZP}{TZ}$
    $\dfrac{12}{10+6} = \dfrac{x}{10}$

17. (2) $\dfrac{BC}{AC} = \dfrac{CD}{CE}$
    $\dfrac{5}{x} = \dfrac{20}{52}$
    $20x = 260$
    $x = \textbf{13 in.}$

18. (4) $\dfrac{\text{man's height}}{\text{man's shadow}} = \dfrac{\text{tree's height}}{\text{tree's shadow}}$
    $\dfrac{6}{4} = \dfrac{x}{36}$
    $\dfrac{216}{4} = \dfrac{4x}{4}$
    $\textbf{54 ft} = x$

19. (2) **angle Q = angle X.** Satisfies SAS requirement.

20. (1) **GI = TU.** Satisfies ASA requirement.

21. (4) $16^2 + 30^2 = d^2$
    $256 + 900 = d^2$
    $1156 = d^2$
    $\textbf{34 ft} = d$

22. (5) One-half of base = 8 in.
    $8^2 + x^2 = 17^2$
    $64 + x^2 = 289$
    $x^2 = 225$
    $x = \textbf{15 in.}$

23. (2) Let d = distance.
    $d^2 + 30^2 = 50^2$
    $d^2 + 900 = 2500$
    $d^2 = 1600$
    $d = \textbf{40 ft}$

24. (4) (10, -4)

25. (2) $A = (-8, 10)$
    $B = (-4, 7)$
    $d = \sqrt{[-4-(-8)]^2 + (7-10)^2}$

Answer Key, Chapter 7, Level 2

18. $c^2 = a^2 + b^2$
$c^2 = 6^2 + 6^2$
$c^2 = 36 + 36$
$c^2 = 72$
$c = \sqrt{36} \cdot \sqrt{2}$
$c = \mathbf{6\sqrt{2}}$ **ft**

19. $c^2 = a^2 + b^2$
$c^2 = 6^2 + 10^2$
$c^2 = 36 + 100$
$c^2 = 136$
$c = \sqrt{4} \cdot \sqrt{34}$
$c = \mathbf{2\sqrt{34}}$ **mi**

20. $c^2 = a^2 + b^2$
$18^2 = 15^2 + b^2$
$324 = 225 + b^2$
$ -225 -225$
$99 = b^2$
$\sqrt{9} \cdot \sqrt{11} = b$
$\mathbf{3\sqrt{11}}$ **yd** $= b$

21. (1) $P = 4s$
$\dfrac{14.92}{4} = \dfrac{4s}{4}$
3.73 ft $= s$

22. (3) $C = \pi d$
$\dfrac{12.56}{3.14} = \dfrac{3.14d}{3.14}$
4 m $= d$

23. (1) $A = lw$
$\dfrac{96}{6} = \dfrac{l \cdot 6}{6}$

24. (5) **Insufficient data is given to solve the problem.** The length of the base is not given.

25. (4) $A = \pi r^2$
$\dfrac{62.8}{3.14} = \dfrac{3.14 r^2}{3.14}$
$\sqrt{\dfrac{\mathbf{62.8}}{\mathbf{3.14}}} = \sqrt{r^2}$

26. (3) Rectangle:
$A = lw$
$A = 8 \times 3$
$A = 24$

Triangle:
$A = \tfrac{1}{2}bh$
$24 = \tfrac{1}{2} \times 12 \times h$
$\dfrac{24}{6} = \dfrac{6h}{6}$
4 ft $= h$

27. (4) $V = lwh$
$360 = l \times 10 \times 9$
$\dfrac{360}{10 \times 9} = \dfrac{l \times 10 \times 9}{10 \times 9}$

28. (2) Let x = length of each of the two shorter sides.
$P = a + b + c$
$40 = 16 + x + x$
$40 = 16 + 2x$
$-16 -16$
$\dfrac{24}{2} = \dfrac{2x}{2}$
12 in. $= x$

29. (1) $P = a + b + c$
third side $= x$
second side $= x + 3$
$79 = 20 + x + 3 + x$
$79 = 23 + 2x$
$-23 -23$
$\dfrac{56}{2} = \dfrac{2x}{2}$
28 in. $= x$

30. (4) $P = 2l + 2w$
$w = x$
$l = 5x - 3$
$\mathbf{126 = 2(5x - 3) + 2x}$

31. (1) $A = lw$
$37.5 = x \cdot 6x$
$\dfrac{37.5}{6} = \dfrac{6x^2}{6}$
$6.25 = x^2$
2.5 in. $= x$

128 Answer Key, Chapter 7, Level 3

32. (4) $P = a + b + c$
$104 = x + 9x + 3x$
$\dfrac{104}{13} = \dfrac{13x}{13}$
$\dfrac{104}{13} = x$
longest side $= 9x = 9 \times \dfrac{104}{13}$

33. (4) $A = \frac{1}{2}bh$
$b = 4x$
$h = 3x$
$24 = \frac{1}{2} \times 4x \times 3x$
$\dfrac{24}{6} = \dfrac{6x^2}{6}$
$4 = x^2$
$2 \text{ in.} = x$
$b = 4x = 4 \times 2 = \mathbf{8 \text{ in.}}$

34. (5) **Insufficient data is given to solve the problem.** The perimeter or the area of the lot is not given.

35. (4) $V = lwh$
$900 = 5 \cdot 4x \cdot 5x$
$\dfrac{900}{100} = \dfrac{100x^2}{100}$
$9 = x^2$
$3 = x$
height $= 5x = 5(3) = \mathbf{15 \text{ in.}}$

36. (3) $P = 2l + 2w$
$111 = 2(x + 5) + 2x$
$111 = 2x + 10 + 2x$
$111 = 4x + 10$
$\dfrac{101}{4} = \dfrac{4x}{4}$
$25.25 = x$
$l = x + 5 = 25.25 + 5 = \mathbf{30.25 \text{ in.}}$

37. (3) $c^2 = a^2 + b^2$
$c^2 = 5^2 + 10^2$
$c^2 = 25 + 100$
$c^2 = 125$
$c = \sqrt{25} \cdot \sqrt{5}$
$c = \mathbf{5\sqrt{5} \text{ in.}}$

38. (5) $c^2 = a^2 + b^2$
$c^2 = 8^2 + 12^2$
$c = \sqrt{8^2 + 12^2}$

39. (5) **Insufficient data is given to solve the problem.** The length of the base of the grandstand is not given.

40. (4) $c^2 = a^2 + b^2$
$c^2 = 9^2 + 13^2$
$c^2 = 81 + 169$
$c^2 = 250$
$c = \sqrt{25} \cdot \sqrt{10}$
$c = \mathbf{5\sqrt{10} \text{ mi}}$

Half-Length Practice Test

1. (4) **$(x - 3)(x + 7)$** The only factors of 21 are 7 and 3. To get the middle term $4x$, 7 must be positive and 3 must be negative.

2. (3) $k^2 + 7k - 30 = 0$
$(k - 3)(k + 10) = 0$

$k + 10 = 0$		$k - 3 = 0$
$\underline{-10\ \ -10}$	or	$\underline{+3\ \ +3}$
$k = -10$		$k = 3$

3. (2) $i = prt$
$i = \dfrac{^8\cancel{\$800}}{1} \times \dfrac{9.5}{\cancel{100}_1} \times \dfrac{3}{1} = \mathbf{\$228}$ or
$i = \$800 \times 0.095 \times 3 = \mathbf{\$228}$

4. (5) **Insufficient data is given to solve the problem.** The time it will take to repay is needed.

5. (2) **B**

6. (1) Triangle DEF is an isosceles triangle, so the measure of angle E is also 50°.
$50° + 50° = 100°$
$180° - 100° = \mathbf{80°}$

7. (3) two size 9 suits: $2 \times 12 = 24$ or
$\dfrac{12}{1} = \dfrac{x}{2}$
$24 = x$

one size 7 skirt: 5
one size 10 dress: 13.5
three size 8 pants: $3 \times 4 = 12$ or
$\dfrac{4}{1} = \dfrac{x}{3}$
$12 = x$
$24 + 5 + 13.5 + 12 = \mathbf{54.5 \text{ yd}}$

22. (4) $4(h + 1) = 48$

23. (2) $4\frac{1}{2} \div 6 = \frac{9}{2} \div \frac{6}{1} = \frac{\cancel{3}\cancel{6}}{2} \times \frac{1}{\cancel{6}_2} = \frac{3}{4}$ **qt** or

$\frac{\text{quarts}}{\text{packages}} \quad \frac{x}{1} = \frac{4\frac{1}{2}}{6}$

$\frac{6x}{6} = \frac{4\frac{1}{2}}{6}$

$x = 4\frac{1}{2} \div 6 = \frac{9}{2} \div \frac{6}{1}$

$= \frac{\cancel{3}\cancel{6}}{2} \times \frac{1}{\cancel{6}_2} = \frac{3}{4}$ **qt**

24. (3) $-1\frac{1}{2}$

25. (4) $(38\% + 3\%) - 11\% = 41\% - 11\% = \mathbf{30\%}$

26. (3) $\frac{33}{100} \times \frac{991}{1} = \frac{33 \times 991}{100}$ or

$\frac{p}{991} = \frac{33}{100}$

$\frac{100p}{100} = \frac{\mathbf{33 \times 991}}{\mathbf{100}}$

27. (5) **Insufficient data is given to solve the problem.** The age of the middle brother or how the age of the middle brother is related to the age of one of the other brothers is needed.

28. (4)
```
       $ 9.17  or
    40)$366.80
       360
        68
        40
       2 80
       2 80
          0
```

$\frac{\text{earnings}}{\text{hours}} \quad \frac{x}{1} = \frac{\$366.80}{40}$

$\frac{40x}{40} = \frac{\$366.80}{40}$

$x = \mathbf{\$9.17}$

29. (2) $82° + 58° = 140°$
$180° - 140° = \mathbf{40°}$

30. (5) $\frac{1}{2}s + 1 > 13$
$\quad\quad -1 \quad -1$
$\overline{2 \cdot \frac{1}{2}s \quad > 12 \cdot 2}$
$\quad s \quad > 24$

25 is the only choice greater than 24.

31. (5) $\frac{\text{candy bars}}{\text{ounces}} \quad \frac{25}{30} = \frac{1}{x}$

$\frac{25x}{25} = \frac{30}{25}$

$x = 1\frac{5}{25} = \mathbf{1\frac{1}{5}}$ **oz**

32. (4) **C, A, D, E, B**

A. $\frac{\cancel{100}^1}{1} \times \frac{20}{\cancel{100}_1} = 20$ or

$\frac{p}{100} = \frac{20}{100}$

$100p = 2000$

$p = 20$

B. $\frac{\cancel{300}^3}{1} \times \frac{18}{\cancel{100}_1} = 54$ or

$\frac{p}{300} = \frac{18}{100}$

$100p = 5400$

$p = 54$

C. $\frac{\cancel{50}^1}{1} \times \frac{\cancel{24}^{12}}{\cancel{100}_2} = 12$ or

$\frac{p}{50} = \frac{24}{100}$

$100p = 1200$

$p = 12$

D. $\frac{\cancel{125}^5}{1} \times \frac{\cancel{28}^7}{\cancel{100}_{4}} = 35$ or

$\frac{p}{125} = \frac{28}{100}$

$100p = 3500$

$p = 35$

E. $\frac{\cancel{700}^7}{1} \times \frac{6}{\cancel{100}_1} = 42$ or

$\frac{p}{700} = \frac{6}{100}$

$100p = 4200$

$p = 42$

33. (4) Angle e = angle a
Angles a and b are supplementary.
$180° - 25° = \mathbf{155°}$

34. (1) $\frac{p}{\$0.29}$

35. (4) **$0.23(q − 1) + $0.29.** The first ounce will always cost $0.29. Every additional ounce $(q − 1)$ will cost $0.23.

132 Answer Key, Full-Length Practice Test

36. (4) **7 and 8**
$7^2 = 49$ and $8^2 = 64$
54 is between 49 and 64.

37. (1) $(40 \times \frac{3}{4}) + (30 \times \frac{1}{4})$
Victoria : Milton :
$d = rt \quad\quad d = rt$
$d = 40 \times \frac{3}{4} \quad d = 30 \times \frac{1}{4}$

38. (4) $8 \times 8 \times 8 \times 8 = 8^4$. The number of people that each apartment can accommodate is unnecessary information.

39. (4) receiving department $= x$
stock department $= 2x$
shipping department $= 2x + 5$
$x + 2x + 2x + 5 = 145$

40. (3) $A = (-4, -1)$
$B = (4, 3)$
$m = \dfrac{3 - (-1)}{4 - (-4)} = \dfrac{4}{8} = \dfrac{1}{2}$

41. (2) $D = (2, 3)$
$E = (6, -7)$
$M = \left(\dfrac{2+6}{2}, \dfrac{3+(-7)}{2}\right)$
$= \left(\dfrac{8}{2}, \dfrac{-4}{2}\right)$
$= (4, -2)$

42. (2) $V = lwh$
$V = 12 \times 4 \times 2$

43. (3) cost of book $= b$
sales tax $= 0.04b$
$b + 0.04b + \$1.85 = \$10.69$
$1.04b + \$1.85 = \$10.69$
$\underline{\quad -\$1.85 \quad\quad - 1.85}$
$\dfrac{1.04b}{1.04} = \dfrac{8.84}{1.04}$
$b = \$8.50$

44. (1) $(e - 2)(e + 9)$ The only factors of 18 that give the middle term of $7e$ are -2 and 9.

45. (5) Triangles PQR and STU are similar triangles.
$\dfrac{QR}{PR} = \dfrac{TU}{SU}$
$\dfrac{QR}{6} = \dfrac{8}{10}$
$\dfrac{10QR}{10} = \dfrac{6 \times 8}{10}$
$QR = \dfrac{6 \times 8}{10}$

46. (4) computers Rick sold $= r$
computers Karen sold $= 3r$
computers Joe sold $= 3r + 8$
$r + 3r + 3r + 8 = 4194$
$7r + 8 = 4194$
$\underline{\quad\quad -8 \quad\quad -8}$
$\dfrac{7r}{7} = \dfrac{4186}{7}$
$r = 598$
$3r + 8 = 3(598) + 8 = \mathbf{1802}$

47. (3) $\$980 - \$539 = \$441$
$\dfrac{\text{savings}}{\text{original}} \quad \dfrac{^9\$\cancel{441}}{_{149}\$\cancel{980}} \times \dfrac{\cancel{100}^5}{1} = \mathbf{45\%}$ or
$\dfrac{441}{980} = \dfrac{r}{100}$
$44{,}100 = 980r$
$45 = r$
Rate is **45%**.

48. (2) $14b^6c$ Divide coefficients; subtract exponents.

49. (4) $c^2 = a^2 + b^2$
$37^2 = a^2 + 35^2$
$37^2 - 35^2 = a^2$
$\sqrt{37^2 - 35^2} = a$

50. (2) 1990: approximately $130 billion
1985: approximately $95 billion
$130 billion – $95 billion = **$35 billion**

51. (2) 3 1975: approximately $30 billion
1985: approximately $95 billion
3 × $30 billion = $90 billion
which is close to $95 billion

52. (2) $\dfrac{\text{chairs}}{\text{hours}} \quad \dfrac{6}{8} = \dfrac{x}{36}$
$216 = 8x$
$27 = x$

Answer Key, Full-Length Practice Test   133

53. (3) Triangle XYZ is an isosceles triangle.
$P = a + b + c$
$P = 3 + 5 + 5 =$ **13 in.**

54. (4) $w^2 + 2w - 48 = 0$
$(w-6)(w+8) = 0$

$w - 6 = 0$ or $w + 8 = 0$
$+6 +6$ $-8-8$
$w = \mathbf{6}$ $w = \mathbf{-8}$

55. (2) $\dfrac{^7\$\cancel{140}}{1} \times \dfrac{\cancel{20}^4}{\cancel{100}_{5\ 1}} = \$28$ or

$\dfrac{p}{\$140} = \dfrac{20}{100}$
$100p = \$2800$
$p = 28$
$\$140 - \$28 = \mathbf{\$112}$

56. (4) $A = 5 \times 7 = 35 \text{ yd}^2$
$c = nr$
$c = 35 \times \$12 = \mathbf{\$420}$

Simulated Test

1. (1) 5 hr 30 min = $5\tfrac{1}{2}$ hr
$d = rt$
$d = 30 \times 5\tfrac{1}{2} = \dfrac{^{15}\cancel{30}}{1} \times \dfrac{11}{\cancel{2}_1} = \mathbf{165 \text{ mi}}$

2. (4) $\dfrac{70}{4} - \dfrac{40}{4}$

15 min = $\tfrac{1}{4}$ hr
$d = rt$
distance of cheetah =
$70 \times \tfrac{1}{4} = \dfrac{70}{4}$
distance of zebra =
$40 \times \tfrac{1}{4} = \dfrac{40}{4}$

3. (2) 9 months = $\tfrac{3}{4}$ year
$i = prt$
$i = \dfrac{^{15}\cancel{30}\ \$\cancel{3000}}{1} \times \dfrac{9}{\cancel{100}_1} \times \dfrac{3}{\cancel{4}_2} =$
$\dfrac{\$405}{2} = \mathbf{\$202.50}$ or
$i = \$3000 \times 0.09 \times 0.75 = \mathbf{\$202.50}$

4. (3) home equity:
$\$65,000 - \$50,000 = \$15,000$
$i = prt$
$i = \dfrac{^{150}\$\cancel{15,000}}{1} \times \dfrac{7}{\cancel{100}_1} \times \dfrac{5}{1} =$
$\mathbf{\$5250}$ or
$i = \$15,000 \times 0.07 \times 5 = \mathbf{\$5250}$

5. (5) Insufficient data is given to solve the problem. The amount of interest or the interest rate for the home equity loan is needed.

6. (2) Triangle KLM is an isosceles triangle.
$P = a + b + c$
$p = 5 + 3 + 3 = \mathbf{11 \text{ ft}}$

7. (1)
$c = nr$
$\dfrac{\$5.60}{8} = \dfrac{8p}{8}$
$\$0.70 = p$

8. (3) hamburgers:
$c = nr$
$c = 6 \times \$2.50 = \$15$
drinks:
$c = nr$
$c = 4 \times \$1 = \$4$
$\$15 + \$4 = \mathbf{\$19}$

9. (4) $\dfrac{\text{hours}}{\text{bookcases}}$ $\dfrac{2.8}{1} = \dfrac{x}{14}$
$2.8 \times 14 = x$
39.2 hr $= x$

10. (3) $\dfrac{\text{employees}}{\text{salary}}$ $\dfrac{68}{\$23,596} = \dfrac{1}{x}$
$\dfrac{68x}{68} = \dfrac{\$23,596}{68}$
$x = \mathbf{\$347}$

11. (5) $V = s^3$
$V = 8^3 = 8 \times 8 \times 8 = \mathbf{512 \text{ in.}^3}$

12. (2) Angles a and h are alternate exterior angles, so the measure of angle h is also 116°. Angles g and h are supplementary angles. 180° − 116° = 64°

13. (3) Measure of the third angle:
80° + 61° = 141°
180° − 141° = 39°
The largest angle measures 80°, and the segment opposite it, **Highway C**, is the longest segment.

134   Answer Key, Full-Length Practice Test; Simulated Test

14. **(4)** $x^2 - 11x - 24 =$
$(-3)^2 - 11(-3) - 24 =$
$9 + 33 - 24 = \textbf{18}$

15. **(4)** 4 lb 4 oz = $4\frac{1}{4}$ lb
Total weight:
$4\frac{1}{4} \times 8 = \frac{17}{\cancel{4}} \times \frac{\cancel{8}^2}{1} = 34$
$c = nr$
$c = 34 \times \$0.40$
$c = \textbf{\$13.60}$

16. **(2)** $\dfrac{\text{cost}}{\text{weeks}}$ $\dfrac{\$59.80}{52} = \dfrac{x}{1}$
$\dfrac{\$59.80}{52} = \dfrac{52x}{52}$
$\textbf{\$1.15} = x$

17. **(2)** Adults: $10\% + 32\% + 19\% = 61\%$
Children or senior citizens:
$7\% + 18\% + 14\% = 39\%$
$61\% - 39\% = \textbf{22\%}$

18. **(4)** $\dfrac{2}{500 - 30}$

19. **(2)** $7m - 3n + 10n - 9m =$
$7m - 9m - 3n + 10n = \textbf{-2m + 7n}$

20. **(1)** 40 min = $\frac{2}{3}$ hr
$d = rt$
$15 = r \cdot \frac{2}{3}$
$\frac{3}{2} \cdot 15 = r \cdot \frac{2}{3} \cdot \frac{3}{2}$
$\frac{45}{2} = r$
$\textbf{22}\frac{1}{2} = r$

21. **(3)** $\dfrac{p}{\$3000} = \dfrac{15}{100}$
$\dfrac{100p}{100} = \dfrac{\$3000 \times 15}{100}$
$p = \dfrac{\$3000 \times 15}{100}$

22. **(4)** $\$37.63 + x = \$148.95$

23. **(1)** $A = \pi r^2$
$\dfrac{153.86}{3.14} = \dfrac{3.14r^2}{3.14}$
$49 = r^2$
$\textbf{7 ft} = r$

24. **(5)** $4x + 0.04(4x) = \$8.52$

25. **(1)** **A**

26. **(2)** $V = \pi r^2 h$
$r = 4 \div 2 = 2$
$V = 3.14 \times 2^2 \times 4$
$V = \textbf{50.24 in.}^3$

27. **(3)** $2t + \$57 = \$135$

28. **(2)** number of years
Roger has worked = r
number of years
Ben has worked = $2r - 3$
$r + 2r - 3 = 54$
$3r - 3 = 54$
$\underline{ +3 +3}$
$\dfrac{3r}{3} = \dfrac{57}{3}$
$r = 19$
$2r - 3 = 2(19) - 3 = 38 - 3 = \textbf{35}$

29. **(3)** Let t = ticket cost
$5t + \$8 = 9t - \$28$
$ +28 +28$
$\overline{5t + \$36 = 9t}$
$-5t -5t$
$\dfrac{\$36}{4} = \dfrac{4t}{4}$
$\textbf{\$9} = t$

30. **(2) B, E, A, C, D**
$\dfrac{1400}{2100} = \dfrac{2}{3} = \dfrac{20}{30}$
$\dfrac{180}{200} = \dfrac{9}{10} = \dfrac{27}{30}$
$\dfrac{18}{36} = \dfrac{1}{2} = \dfrac{15}{30}$
$\dfrac{8}{20} = \dfrac{2}{5} = \dfrac{12}{30}$
$\dfrac{100}{120} = \dfrac{5}{6} = \dfrac{25}{30}$

31. **(3)** $c = \sqrt{30^2 + 25^2}$

32. **(5)** $\dfrac{\text{length}}{\text{width}}$ $\dfrac{12}{8} = \dfrac{5}{x}$
$12x = 8 \times 5$
$x = \dfrac{\textbf{8} \times \textbf{5}}{\textbf{12}}$

Answer Key, Simulated Test

33. **(5)**
$$\frac{1}{3}h - 2 \geq 7$$
$$\phantom{\frac{1}{3}h}+2 +2$$
$$3 \cdot \frac{1}{3}h \geq 9 \cdot 3$$
$$h \geq 27$$

27 is the only choice greater than or equal to 27.

34. **(3)** 1985: approximately 106
1989: approximately 123
123 − 106 = **17**

35. **(1) Both houses are the same distance from the barn.** The third angle of the triangle measures 61°: 180° − (58° + 61°) = 61°. An isosceles triangle is formed, meaning the legs are of equal length.

36. **(3)**
$$c^2 = a^2 + b^2$$
$$50^2 = 40^2 + b^2$$
$$2500 = 1600 + b^2$$
$$-1600 \quad -1600$$
$$900 = b^2$$
$$\mathbf{30\ ft} = b$$

37. **(4)** cans × base × height × stores =
12 × 12 × 12 × 12 = **12⁴**

38. **(3)** 8.654 × 10⁵ = 8.654 × 100,000 = **865,400**

39. **(5)** $5\frac{5}{8} \div 6 = \frac{\cancel{45}^{15}}{8} \times \frac{1}{\cancel{6}_2} = \frac{15}{16}$ **acres**

40. **(4)**
```
    1050
    1100
    1230
     980
     950
    1100
 +  1290
    ————
    7700
```

$$\begin{array}{r} 1100 \\ 7\overline{)7700} \end{array}$$

41. **(5) Insufficient data is given to solve the problem.** The number of prizes to be awarded is not given.

42. **(1)** Denver passengers: approximately 32 million

$$\frac{\overset{8}{\cancel{32}}}{1} \times \frac{65}{\cancel{100}_{25}} = \frac{520}{25} = 20.8 \text{ or}$$

$$\frac{p}{32} = \frac{65}{100}$$
$$100p = 2080$$
$$p = 20.8$$
$$32 - 20.8 = \mathbf{11.2}$$

43. **(2) Chicago to London**
Chicago passengers: approximately 57 million
London passengers: approximately 38 million

$$\frac{\text{Chicago}}{\text{London}} \quad \frac{57 \text{ million}}{38 \text{ million}} = \frac{3}{2}$$

44. **(4)** $V = lwh$
$V = \mathbf{(10)(15)(9)}$

45. **(2)** Amy = x
Brian = $x + 4$
Mary = $2x - 3$
$x + x + 4 + 2x - 3 = 25$
$4x + 1 = 25$
$ -1 -1$
$\frac{4x}{4} = \frac{24}{4}$
$x = 6$
$2x - 3 = 2(6) - 3 = 12 - 3 = \mathbf{9}$

46. **(4)** $A = (0, 1)$
$C = (2, -9)$
$m = \frac{(-9-1)}{(2-0)} = \frac{-10}{2} = \mathbf{-5}$

47. **(1)** $E = (-4, 9)$
$D = (8, 5)$
$M = \left(\frac{-4+8}{2}, \frac{9+5}{2}\right)$
$= \left(\frac{4}{2}, \frac{14}{2}\right)$
$= \mathbf{(2, 7)}$

48. **(4)** Radius of larger circle:
2 × 6 = 12 in.
Diameter of larger circle:
2 × 12 = **24 in.**

136   Answer Key, Simulated Test

49. (4) $\dfrac{\text{bush's shadow}}{\text{bush's height}} = \dfrac{\text{tree's shadow}}{\text{tree's height}}$

$$\dfrac{10}{12} = \dfrac{45}{x}$$

$$10x = 540$$

$$x = \mathbf{54\ ft}$$

50. (4) $t^2 + 15t + 56 = 0$

$(t+7)(t+8) = 0$

$\begin{array}{rlcrl} t+7 &= 0 & & t+8 &= 0 \\ \underline{-7} & \underline{-7} & \text{or} & \underline{-8} & \underline{-8} \\ t &= -7 & & t &= \mathbf{-8} \end{array}$

51. (2) $\mathbf{6fh^5}$. Divide coefficients; subtract exponents.

52. (1) Withholding 24% of her monthly income of $1850 for taxes

Choice 1:

$\dfrac{^{37}\cancel{\$1850}}{1} \times \dfrac{\cancel{24}^{12}}{\cancel{100}_{\cancel{2}_1}} = \$444$ or

$\dfrac{p}{\$1850} = \dfrac{24}{100}$

$100p = \$44,400$

$p = \$444$

Choice 2:
$360

Choice 3:

$\dfrac{1}{_1\cancel{48}} \times \dfrac{\cancel{\$11,568}^{241}}{1} = \$241$

Choice 4:

$\dfrac{1}{_1\cancel{12}} \times \dfrac{\cancel{\$3900}^{325}}{1} = \$325$

Choice 5:
$220 \times \$1.50 = \$330$

53. (2) $\$1400 - \$952 = \$448$

$\dfrac{\text{savings}}{\text{list price}}$ $\dfrac{\$448}{_{14}\cancel{\$1400}} \times \dfrac{\cancel{100}^1}{1} = \mathbf{32\%}$

or

$\dfrac{\$448}{\$1400} = \dfrac{r}{100}$

$\$44,800 = \$1400r$

$32 = r$ Rate is **32%**.

54. (2) $4(6 \times \$0.25 + \$0.75) - \$6.75$

Multiply the cost of buying the paper at the newsstand for a week times 4. Then subtract the delivered cost for 4 weeks, $6.75, from this.

55. (4) $d = rt$

$\dfrac{300}{45} = \dfrac{45t}{45}$

$6\dfrac{2}{3}\ \mathbf{hr} = t$

56. (5) $\dfrac{\text{hours}}{\text{earnings}}$ $\dfrac{40}{\$330} = \dfrac{27}{x}$

$40x = \$330 \times 27$

Formulas

Description	Formula
AREA (A) of a:	
square	$A = s^2$; where s = side
rectangle	$A = lw$; where l = length, w = width
parallelogram	$A = bh$; where b = base, h = height
triangle	$A = \frac{1}{2}bh$; where b = base, h = height
circle	$A = \pi r^2$; where π = 3.14, r = radius
PERIMETER (P) of a:	
square	$P = 4s$; where s = side
rectangle	$P = 2l + 2w$; where l = length, w = width
triangle	$P = a + b + c$; where $a, b,$ and c are the sides
circumference (C) of a circle	$C = \pi d$; where π = 3.14, d = diameter
VOLUME (V) of a:	
cube	$V = s^3$; where s = side
rectangular container	$V = lwh$; where l = length, w = width, h = height
cylinder	$V = \pi r^2 h$; where π = 3.14, r = radius, h = height
Pythagorean relationship	$c^2 = a^2 + b^2$; where c = hypotenuse, a and b are legs of a right triangle
distance (d) between two points in a plane	$d = \sqrt{(x_2 - x_1)^2 + (y_2 - y_1)^2}$; where (x_1, y_1) and (x_2, y_2) are two points in a plane
slope of a line (m)	$m = \frac{y_2 - y_1}{x_2 - x_1}$; where (x_1, y_1) and (x_2, y_2) are two points in a plane
mid point of a line	$M = \left(\frac{x_1 + x_2}{2}, \frac{y_1 + y_2}{2}\right)$
mean	mean = $\frac{x_1 + x_2 + \cdots + x_n}{n}$; where the x's are the values for which a mean is desired, and n = number of values in the series
median	median = the point in an ordered set of numbers at which half of the numbers are above and half of the numbers are below this value
simple interest (i)	$i = prt$, where p = principal, r = rate, t = time
distance (d) as function of rate and time	$d = rt$; where r = rate, t = time
total cost (c)	$c = nr$; where n = number of units, r = cost per unit